# THE
# SEVERN VALLEY

## WALKS FOR MOTORISTS

Peter A. Price

30 Walks with sketch maps

**COUNTRYSIDE BOOKS**
NEWBURY, BERKSHIRE

*Countryside Books' walking guides cover most areas of England and Wales and include the following series:*

*County Rambles*
*Walks For Motorists*
*Exploring Long Distance Paths*
*Literary Walks*

*A complete list is available from the publishers.*

First Published 1981
by Frederick Warne Ltd.

This completely revised and updated edition
published 1991
© Peter A. Price 1991

COUNTRYSIDE BOOKS
3 Catherine Road
Newbury, Berkshire

ISBN 1 85306 112 3

Cover photograph taken by Andy Williams

## PUBLISHERS' NOTE

While every care has been taken in the compilation of this book, the publishers cannot accept responsibility for any inaccuracies. But things may have changed since the book was published; paths are sometimes diverted, a concrete bridge may replace a wooden one, stiles disappear.

The length of each walk is given in miles and kilometres, but within the text imperial measurements are quoted. It is useful to bear the following approximations in mind: 5 miles = 8 kilometres, ½ mile = 805 metres, 1 metre = 39.4 inches.

Produced through MRM Associates Ltd., Reading
Printed by J.W. Arrowsmith Ltd., Bristol

# Contents

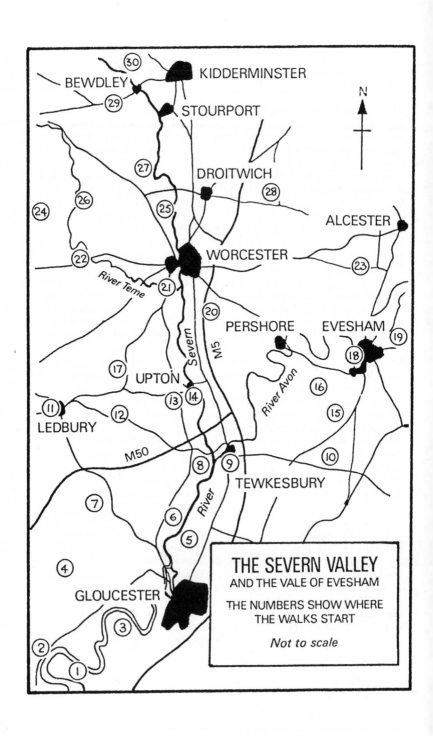

# Introduction

The Severn Valley, from Slimbridge in the south to Bewdley and the Wyre Forest in the north, is steeped in history. Since the diversion of the river southwards, away from the Dee estuary, at the end of the last Ice Age, man has been able to use it as the main artery into the heart of the country. It was often easier to ship heavy loads by water because of the poor condition of the roads. The 30 large prehistoric camps which look down on the wide fertile valley still proclaim that man has toiled here for many thousands of years. Each generation has left its mark— sometimes only faintly—to add a feeling of continuity to the landscape. The historian, Dr Hoskins, author of *The Making of the English Landscape*, likens the understanding of the English landscape to the appreciation of music—the themes as they enter or recur affect the quality of the whole. Nowhere can this be seen better than in the Severn Valley, where the Severn and its two great tributaries, the (Stratford) Avon and the Teme, provide a link between prehistoric man and the pleasure boats of today.

The Severn Valley is bounded on the east by the limestone escarpment of the Cotswolds and in the west by the Old Red Sandstone of Herefordshire. The plain is overlaid in many places by alluvium and glacial deposits but the eastern half is Lower Jurassic and the western half Mesozoic Trias. The Malvern Hills on the western side, apart from providing excellent hill walking, give us a convenient glimpse of rocks thrust up from deep in the earth's crust.

The hedgerows in the lowland farmland are rich in wild flowers. Those who like to vary their diet by the use of wild foods may know that it is safe to eat chickweed, which is abundant; add a little yarrow and a few dandelion leaves and you have a welcome addition to bread and cheese. In autumn blewets and the stately parasol mushroom are in the fields and the bitter sloe hangs from many of the hedges. The pheasant is sometimes disturbed and flocks of lapwing range over the riverside meadows. The comma butterfly, which lays its eggs on hops and nettles, is sometimes seen and the salmon negotiating the weirs as it makes its way upstream is a thrilling sight.

To get the most out of these walks—or any walk—it is necessary to put more in than just walking-power. It is hoped that the observations made along the way will help to make the walks more interesting. Much more could be mentioned but space will not allow.

All walks in this book are circular; they start and finish at the same place. The routes described are on public rights-of-way as shown on the Definitive Map or the County Road Record or are on Forestry Commission land to which the public have access. 'Members of the Public are permitted to enter Forestry Commission land entirely at their own risk on condition that they will have no claim whatsoever against the Forestry Commission for any loss, damage or injury howsoever suffered or caused.' Some of the walks go through farmland or private woodland which is the source of income to the farmer. Damage to fences, walls or gates—apart from the expense involved in repairs—may cause suffering to animals who could get out and eat the wrong food or be injured by a car.

Make sure you observe the country code:
Guard against fire risk
Fasten all gates
Keep dogs under proper control
Keep to the paths across farmland
Avoid damaging fences, hedges and walls
Leave no litter
Safeguard water supplies
Protect wild life, wild plants and trees
Go carefully on country roads
Respect the life of the countryside

The most important item of equipment for the walker is footwear. You may come across quite a lot of mud even in summer so the best protection is to have a lightweight pair of boots. Most walkers get them a size too big and then wear an extra pair of thick socks to stop the boots rubbing. When turned down over the top of the boot the socks will stop small stones getting down under the feet. When you get back to the car you can take the boots off and change back to clean shoes. Boots are also advisable when the ground is hard and dry because the muddy gateways and tracks dry into very uneven ground and it is easy to twist an ankle in an unguarded moment.

A map is not strictly necessary if this guide is carried as the routes are described in detail and sketch maps are provided. An Ordnance Survey map, however, adds interest and helps to identify points in distant prospects that are not mentioned in the text. Such maps also show the local roads. You will find the number of the appropriate Ordnance Survey Landranger and Pathfinder Sheets which cover the area concerned, together with the map reference of the start, are given at the beginning of each walk.

If a right-of-way in the county of Hereford and Worcester is found to be obstructed, it would be helpful if details of the obstruction, together with its location, were reported to the Secretary and Solicitor, Hereford and Worcester County Council, County Hall, Spetchley Road, Worcester.

# ARLINGHAM

## WALK 1

★

8½ miles (14 km)

OS Landranger 162, Pathfinder SO 61/71

The village of Arlingham is in the centre of a large loop of the river Severn. It is 6 miles north of the Slimbridge Wildfowl Trust and 9 miles south-west of Gloucester. Much of the walk is along the edge of the river which here is wide, with many large sandbanks.

From Junction 13 on the M5 go towards Slimbridge for 1 mile and leave the A38 at the sign for Frampton and Saul. In 1½ miles pass the end of the Frampton-on-Severn village green and go over the Gloucester and Sharpness Canal. Just past the canal swing-bridge the main road turns sharp right towards Saul. Here go straight ahead towards Fretherene and Arlingham. Pass the church on the left opposite the first turn and take the next turn to follow the sign 'Overton Lane'. Go up the hill, past the farm at the top on the left, and park the car on the wide grass verge, clear of any gateway, anywhere in the next ½ mile. (GR: SO 732 106)

Over to the left is Wick Court, a very interesting medieval moated manor house. It is said that Queen Elizabeth I visited it on one of her progressions. There is a well preserved sixteenth century house with some outbuildings surrounded by a moat. Moated sites, and there are many hundreds in the west of the country, have usually lost their buildings and all that remains is part of the ditchwork in an overgrown corner of a field. The house is in private hands but a conducted tour may be arranged by telephoning Gloucester 741304 in advance.

The Severn bore, which you may chance to see during this walk, comes in three sizes—small, medium and large—though it occurs on only 130 of the 365 days in the year. The bore starts when the tide comes into the constricted river at Sharpness and rushes into the wider channel of Frampton Sand where it passes over a sloping floor which is a continuation of the rocks at Hock Cliff (seen later in the walk). This causes a wave to form at the tide's leading edge and both wave and rush of water surge upstream, filling the river. A large bore is a most impressive sight, especially nearer to Gloucester where it can be as high as 9 feet and travelling at 13 mph. Before the tide comes in, the river here flows between wide mud flats, consequently the bore is only low,

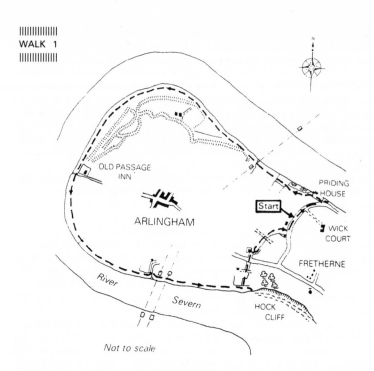

Not to scale

but after the bore is past, the river runs in reverse and quickly fills up. An information sheet is issued by the Heart of England Tourist Board (PO Box 15. Worcester) which gives details on when and where to see the bore at its best.

Walk on down the lane to the sharp right hand bend in front of Priding House. Turn left here as directed by a footpath sign indicating The Severn Way. This is a walk devised by Gloucestershire County Council and follows the river from Tewkesbury to below Sharpness.

Follow the path along the very edge of the bank. It is liable to flooding when there is a high tide but the path at the top of the bank on the left is less muddy.

In spring this is a good spot for elver fishing. In March and April young eels, known as elvers, swim up the river. They have spent three years drifting across the Atlantic Ocean from deep in the sea off the continental shelf of Central America where they were spawned. At this time of the year they enter the Severn in great shoals and local

8

fishermen still make a good income from a few hours' fishing. The elver-net, about 3 feet long, 2 feet wide and 18 inches deep, is set on a pole 4 or 5 feet long. The time of fishing is of paramount importance as it is at the turn of the tide that the elvers swim upstream in huge numbers. Standing on the shore, the fisherman dips his net into the river and after a few moments, with a gentle sweep, empties it into a waiting bucket strategically placed 2 yards up the bank. From a good handful to a quart is taken at each dip and the bucket is soon full of frothing, translucent, worm-like creatures barely 3 inches long. They are usually cooked alive in bacon fat, when they turn white and look very much like spaghetti with eyes!

In just over ¼ mile the path leaves the high bank and follows the edge of the river. On approaching the tall power-cable mast, go over a narrow stream by a bridge and continue near the river to the riverside bank. Flooding has always been a problem to the farmers on the river terraces which border the Severn and each age has had to build new, or strengthen the old, flood prevention banks. The most recent ones are those which follow the river bank, so protecting all but a narrow strip on the riverside. Older ones protected the cultivated land only; they therefore followed the edge of the ridge and furrow, many of which can still be seen. Consequently the old banks, like the 'drunken English roads', twist and turn, often going far inland.

Keep to the flood bank for 3½ miles to the Old Passage Inn. Before the Severn Bridge was built, not so long ago, this was the first place up the river where a crossing could be made. It was a difficult and dangerous way to get to and from South Wales but the first bridge upstream was at Gloucester, which meant a long detour. It is said that after the battle of Deorham (Dyrham) in AD 577 the defeated Britons fled from the Saxons to this crossing. When the Saxons arrived they saw the Britons retreating across the river and—not knowing the river—tried to cut them off by running across upstream. But this is the most dangerous reach of the Severn, with many whirlpools and undercur-rents, and many Saxons perished.

Continue the walk along the riverside flood bank. For the next mile much of the old winding bank has been replaced by a new, gently curving one. The point where the next large stream flows into the river is called Hope Pill. A 'pill' is the mouth of a tide-washed brook. Walk on along the flood bank, climbing up the side of a field in one place to avoid some low cliffs, almost as far as Hock Cliff, topped by one of the few woods on the peninsula.

Hock Cliff is of great interest to geologists, for here bands of hard limestone about 1 foot thick are set in bands of thinly laminated soft shales. Usually, when this occurs, it is grassed over and cannot be seen. It is over similar steps out in the river bed that the incoming tide rushes

9

to form the bore. It is also from these cliffs that the finest examples of the fossil Gryphaea Arcuata (commonly known as the Devil's toenail) are to be found. Other fossils include Belemnites which look like bullets and Sea Lilies (Pentacrinus), the stems of which are made up from dozens of small 5-pointed sections.

This is the end of the riverside walking. It is now necessary to walk inland for just over ½ a mile back to the car. To do this, turn left at the second stile on the left. With your back to the river and the hedge on the left, walk to an elbow in the hedge and then continue with the hedge on the right. Go through the right-hand of 2 gates in the hedge at the far end of the field. Follow the track beyond with a hedge on the left and a ditch on the right to the road. Continue ahead towards 2 cottages and follow the lane round to the right as far as the entrance to a house. On the left of the garden gates you will see a stile in the hedge. Go over the stile and turn right to follow the hedge up the fields, crossing a farm track in 100 yards, to a stile in the top hedge. On the road beyond turn left and pass the farm on the left, at the top of the hill, which you passed in the car just before starting the walk.

# NEWNHAM

## WALK 2

★

5½ miles (9 km)

OS Landranger 162, Pathfinder SO 61/71

This walk climbs up over 600 feet to the edge of the Forest of Dean where there is a view point called Blaize Bailey. On the way up and back the route goes through farmland where there may be some mud in wet weather.

Newnham is on the A48(T) road, 10 miles south-west of Gloucester and 15 miles north of junction 22 on the M4 at Chepstow.

Cars can be parked in the official car park at the northern end of Newnham. (GR: SO 693 120). This car park, with toilets, is next to the river and is popular with fishermen and those who come to watch the Severn bore, for here you can see the bore go past and then you can drive along the A48 to Minsterworth and see it again. By car you do the journey in 10 minutes but the bore, which has to go more than twice as far, takes 60 minutes.

The town of Newnham has a long and varied history. It was from here that Richard le Clare, Earl of Pembroke (Strongbow), sailed in 1171 to conquer Ireland. In the seventeenth and eighteenth centuries it was the port for Flexley's iron. Later, when Dean ore ran out, Lancashire ore came in for the many furnaces in Dean. From 1276 it was a market for leather, there being two large tanneries there, one to the south west of the town and one in the middle. Tanning used oak bark, from trees felled in April or May, which was carted from Dean. When it arrived in the yard it was powdered and put into vats. The skins were cleaned of hairs after soaking in lime pits for 6 weeks and were then put in the tanning pits. The process took up to 3 years and the stench was tremendous—perhaps one of the most polluting activities man could devise. Gardeners will be interested to know that more than 350 years ago, in Newnham, Sir Edward Mansell built the first greenhouse. The glass came from a small glass works in the town and the coal to heat it from Dean by packhorse.

Leave the car park and walk along the pavement of the main road into Newnham. In a few yards, at the large left-hand bend, cross the road and go up a 'No through road'. In 100 yards turn left over a stile, next to

11

DEAN
HILL

LITTLE
HYDE

Start

BLAIZE
BAILEY

BESSY'S
WOOD

NEWNHAM

River Severn

*Not to scale*

the entrance to Whetstones, into the corner of a field and follow the
hedge on the left to the road through a housing estate. Turn left and at
the T-junction with Hyde Lane turn right. Follow this lane over the
railway bridge, with the entrance to the tunnel away to the left, and
then bear round to the right. After passing the last house walk along the
raised grass verge. When this ends the right of way goes straight ahead
over a stile and then to the left almost as far as the brow of the hill where
it turns right across the field to go down to a footbridge. Cross the
narrow strip of grass to the track to Little Hyde. (Much, but not all, of
this walk follows a waymark with a black spot, a Forest of Dean walk.)
On the other side of the track, a few yards to the left, a stile marks the
beginning of a footpath across the field to a stile a little to the right of
Little Hyde. It is in line with the electricity pole. Now cross the narrow
neck of field to another stile 50 yards from the left-hand corner.

Beyond is a large field which was formerly three smaller fields. Go
straight ahead down the middle of the field to pass through a wide gap
where there used to be a continuous hedge. Now bear right to a stile,
100 yards to the right of the opposite corner. From here go ahead to
another stile and then keep this direction in the next field as far as a
sunken track, the remains of an old Dean road, and turn left.

As with many old roads when they go up the hillside, a footpath went
up the adjoining pasture. Hills to a lorry or bus mean nothing but a

12

change of gears and an increase in fuel consumption, but to a horse with a waggon it meant a great strain. All people were required to get off the waggon to lighten the load and as the roads were deeply rutted and very muddy most of the year, they walked up the hill in the fields beside the road—unless they had to help by pushing! There is a footpath up the hill next to the hedge on the left whilst the old road is still a bridleway.

Continue up the bridleway and then a lane. This comes to a T-junction with the road from Newnham to Littledean, turn left. Cross the road so as to face the oncoming traffic and in 200 yards fork right along a 'No through road' which is a continuation of the sunken track followed on the way up. In 100 yards, at the fork, keep straight ahead, with Temple Farm on the right. In front, to the left of the lane, there is a stile into a field. Along this footpath, which follows the lane hedge, there is a magnificent view to the east.

Walk 1 can be traced almost entirely, from its beginning on the left of the Arlingham peninsula, round from left to right near the river, to the cliffs beyond the twin pylons and back across the higher ground. Gloucester is 10 miles away over the left-hand bend of the river and Slimbridge 5 miles away over the right. A few yards short of the house there is a stile which takes you into the lane.

Follow the lane to a small green with a few scattered houses and bear right to the entrance to the forest. Here you go through the widest kissing gate between Wye and Thames. In 50 yards bear left up a dusty forest road. This is part of a drive for motorists to use to reach the view point. All traffic will approach you from behind, so keep to the side. Follow the signs to the view point.

Walk along the forest road which goes down the hill from the view point. It is the practice of the Forestry Commission to allow the deciduous indigenous trees of the area to develop on the edges of plantations. This softens the effect of dark rows of conifers, which provide the Commission's main income. We are therefore able to enjoy beech, birch and the sallow, whose large catkins, appearing before the leaves, provide bees with their first feast of the year.

In ¼ mile the track levels off at a wide grass area. Here bear slightly left down an old track, leaving the main track to sweep round to the right. In 100 yards turn left at a cross-track which soon comes up to a deserted settlement. There are the remains of a number of houses in the wood on the left, which suggests that this was a busy little place not so very long ago.

Pass the farm and cottages, now all deserted and beginning to fall down. Go through a gate and after a short length of hedged track, continue across the field, turning right in front of some old barns. In a few yards turn left down the side of the end barn. Here you leave the Black Spot Waymark which goes off to the right. Go straight across the field and about half way across you will notice a ditch starting to form. This develops into a sunken track which should be followed down the side of the hill. At the end of the wood turn left and in 20 yards go over a stile. In the next field bear right across the head of a little valley and go towards Bessy's wood. Walk down the side of the wood to the corner where there is a stile. From here turn left and with a fence on the left go down the hill for ¾ mile to a stile on the left a few yards before a gate. The path goes straight across the bottom of an old pear orchard. Newnham was famous for its perry in the seventeenth and eighteenth centuries. Connoisseurs maintained that it was possible to say from which orchard the fruit came—just as now they claim to identify the vineyard from which a wine comes. Today all pears are mixed together and so the subtle flavours are lost.

Just past the gateway turn right and, aiming for the large white house across the valley, cross the field to a railway bridge. From the bridge can be seen, in one direction, the other end of the tunnel seen on the way out; in the other, a view down the valley. The buildings on the left of the track, ¼ mile away, were originally a tannery. Cross the next field to the top right-hand corner to a sunken track and then out to the road. Here turn right and walk along The Green, a small park of which any town could be proud, to the main road.

A quick walk along the main street to the left will bring you back to the car in a few moments. A slower walk will be rewarding, for Newnham is a well kept place with many hidden treasures. For example, a short walk through the churchyard opposite will offer you a superb view of the river from the top of a cliff. The first church was further to the east than the present one but as the cliff was eroded, the church was lost. The second was destroyed by fire. Slowly but surely the river is at work at the base of the cliff and some day another church would have been needed but for the work of the River Authority, who are present building a wall at the base of the cliff.

# ELMORE

## WALK 3

★

5½ miles (9 km)

OS Landranger 162, Pathfinder SO 61/71

Elmore is 3 miles south-west of Gloucester. It is reached by turning off the old A38, which is now the B4008, at Quedgeley or Hardwick. Cross the Gloucester and Sharpness Canal near the Pilot Inn and in ½ mile bear right for Elmore. Pass the turning on the right to Stonebench and continue for 1 mile. Half a mile past the entrance to Elmore Court turn left down a 'No through road', signposted to Keepers Lodge and Velthouse Farm and, in 20 yards, park on the right. (GR: SO 776 148)

Elmore Court has belonged to the Guise family since the thirteenth century and the present house dates from 1588. The wrought-iron gates were first erected at Rencombe, near Cirencester, in 1712 and brought here in the early nineteenth century. Notice the acanthus and hearts-tongue fern in the design. The Court is usually open to the public on the first Sunday in the month during summer.

Go down the lane away from the signpost and in 100 yards bear left. In a further 300 yards, where there is a gentle rise in the road and a cottage can be seen 100 yards ahead, turn left through a gate in a wire fence. Bear slightly left from this gate to another gate across the field and then continue with the hedge on the left. In the third field bear slightly right to a gateway 100 yards from the corner. From here look across the next field and you will see a stile in the opposite hedge. Go to this and then bear right to a gate near an angle in the right-hand hedge. Immediately beyond this gate turn left and go towards a house in the distance. As you near the far end of the field bear left to a gate which leads out to the lane. Turn left and in 100 yards bear right down a narrow lane to Wier Green.

Walk down the lane to the river and turn left over a stile on the left with a signpost 'The Severn Way'. As you walk along the riverside here you are in the old orchards which produced an important part of the income of the farmers and cottagers in past centuries. To the left, at the end of the orchards, is Windmill Hill. Alas, the windmill is no longer there. The river soon curves round to the left on a stretch known as Madam's Pool.

Follow the river downstream for a mile to Elmore Back, a hamlet strung out along slightly higher ground than the fields behind. Keep near the river bank and go along the flood bank between the orchards and the river. Between Elmore Back and Minsterworth there is a submerged line of rock on which, in the past, it was possible to walk across the river at low tide. Fragments of the outcrop of rock can be seen in the bank near Minsterworth church. Continue along the river bank. Two hundred yards past the last farmhouse you will see a small building belonging to the South Gloucestershire Internal Drainage Board. It is the Elmore Back Pumping Station and is responsible for lifting the water out of the ditch into the river.

Walk on along the bank to the end of the next large field and stop. Away in front can be seen the few surviving trees of an old orchard. The new flood defences have swept away the remains of the building which once stood where you are now standing. This was The Shark, a notorious cider house, which was well known in the seventeenth and eighteenth centuries and was hidden by orchards. Here river traffic would stop to enable the crews to sample the local brew—and sometimes leave a few kegs of French brandy. This was in the days when

16

cider and perry were sent to London, where it was valued as European wine is today. Who would notice a keg of brandy in a waggon-load of cider barrels?

From here you turn left through a gate, treading in the footsteps of the smugglers as they started on their way to London. Walk along the side of the field, having the ditch and hedge on your right, to a gate in the corner. On the track beyond, turn right into the corner of a field and follow the hedge on the left for 50 yards round to a gate. In the next field walk with the hedge on the right. In the first corner turn left and keep this direction for 1 mile. You will go through two gates and then an orchard. The track then becomes a raised causeway as it crosses the low-lying ground.

At various places along the causeway, where the edges have been broken down into the ditch, the original road surface can be seen. This consists of flat stone laid on edge. Each stone was laid in position by hand! Because only the edges took the pressure there was no chance of the stones tipping or moving. The causeway eventually rises up through a field to a lane at Farley's End. At the lane turn left.

In 200 yards bear right and in a further ¼ mile you come to the turning to Keepers Lodge, where the car is parked.

# GLASSHOUSE

## WALK 4

★

5 miles (8 km)

OS Landranger 162, Pathfinder SO 62/72

This walk climbs up over 700 feet to the top of May Hill and much of it is through the famous Newent Wood. In spring these woods are filled with wild daffodils and bluebells.

Glasshouse is 3 miles south of Newent and 8 miles west of Gloucester. It is reached from Newent by going out of the centre of the town along Watery Lane, following the signpost to the Falconry Centre and going straight through Clifford's Mesne. From the A40(T) follow the signposts near Huntley or Dursley Cross. The walk starts from the Glasshouse Inn, which stands almost on its own at the foot of May Hill, whilst most of the houses are scattered higher up the hillside.

It was to the large field, which can be seen from the Glasshouse Inn, that the glassmakers of Lorraine came at the beginning of the seventeenth century, bringing their skills to England where glass was coming into more general use. By the end of the century the demand was oustripping supply, which was governed by the amount of charcoal which could be obtained from Newent Wood, so a move to a district where coal was available became necessary. Staffordshire was chosen, thus founding the present-day high class glass industry of that area. The works at Glasshouse were established along the banks of a small stream, now piped underground, which ran down the middle of the large field opposite the manor house. The site of the glass works can be seen by crossing the road bridge opposite the inn and following the lane for 100 yards to Clifford's Mesne (to where a stream flows under the road), and then looking down the field on the right.

Cars may be parked on the grass opposite the Glasshouse Inn. (GR: SO 709 213)

Stand on the green facing the Glasshouse Inn and then go down a track to the right of it, opposite the yew house. At the bottom of the hill the track goes past a cottage with an interesting garden and into Castle Hill Wood. Continue for 200 yards and then turn left and follow a track through the wood. This track winds along and passes a turning on the left after 100 yards. As the path rises up and turns round to the right it

18

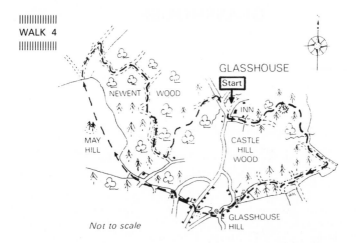

*Not to scale*

goes past the edge of Castle Mound on the right. The ditch and bank of a small motte and bailey can just be seen through the trees.

Go on down to the bottom of the wood and then follow the track ahead, which is just inside the wood. The track rises and then goes on as if to go out of the wood through a gate. Twenty yards before reaching this gate turn back to the right up the hill. At the next junction turn left and then in 20 yards turn right to continue up the hill. In a further 100 yards turn right, do not go ahead out into the corner of a field. When the old track bears right, keep straight ahead. As you go up you can see an overgrown hollow-way on the right. On reaching a field at the top of the rise, keep straight ahead passing to the right of the building to join a track. In a few yards continue with the hedge on the left out to Glasshouse Hill.

At the lane turn left and go down the hill. In 200 yards turn right round a pond along a track. Just past the cottage, where the track narrows, turn right into a field. Go up the field, an old orchard, to a stile in the top right-hand corner. Bear right in the lane beyond and continue up the hill, first on a track and then a muddy, hedged path.

At the next lane turn right for 20 yards and then left, again following a muddy hedged track. Keep the same direction at the cross-paths and, passing the National Trust notice on the left, follow the clear path up to the top of May Hill.

May Hill is a dome of very old rock similar to the sandstone of West Malvern (see Walk 17). From the clump of pine trees at the highest point, 971 feet, there is a view to the west into the mountains of Wales and to the east along the edge of the Cotswolds.

To continue the walk, return to the grass track you came up and follow it along the hill. It gradually goes down and in ½ mile comes to a field gate with a modern gate on the right. In the rough land beyond, bear right down a grass track through the bracken. In ¼ mile, just after a fork in the track, turn right along a track which comes back along the hillside and leads into Newent Wood. This ancient wood still covers nearly 1,000 acres and is famous for its beautiful wild flowers. Just inside the wood bear left along the main track. As you go down you will find short muddy stretches—which have not been improved by horses using the path in winter. In ¼ mile the track forks, one track going on down and the other keeping along the side of the hill. Go right and at the next cross-tracks turn right up the hill.

A narrow strip of coppiced chestnut can be seen on the left. This is a remnant of an older woodland management. As you will have seen around you, commercial woodland today tends to be planted with rows of similar-looking conifers (softwood trees), which grow very quickly and can be used by industry. Softwoods have long fibres and this makes them good for paper-making—up to half the world's wood is used in this way.

Sweet chestnut is a broadleaved tree (hardwood). It is known to have been planted extensively by the Romans and the well-known nuts formed a staple food for their legionaries. A small pole of chestnut contains a great deal of heartwood, so when cleft it lasts well out of doors and is therefore ideal for small fencing. County councils erect miles of chestnut fencing in the fields parallel to main roads to act as snow-breaks. These can be seen in winter on the north side of many of the exposed roads over the Cotswolds. It takes one acre of coppice to supply enough wood for one mile of fence. The large chestnut poles are used in the hopyards and the small ones for making walking sticks. Coppicing is the process of cutting down a tree near the ground and allowing the stumps to grow a number of shoots which are left for 10 or 20 years and then cut down. This process can be repeated over and over again.

Continue the walk and in 100 yards bear left along the hillside again. When the track sweeps to the right round the head of a valley, go straight ahead, cutting off the loop of the track. About 100 yards along the track turn left and in 5 yards bear right on to a green track. This is an old forest road used by horses and it eventually re-joins the track. A gate out of the wood soon comes into view but 10 yards before reaching this gate turn left down a grass track which winds its way down through the wood.

As you near the bottom always choose the path to the right downhill. On arriving at the lane turn right.

In front of you is the Glasshouse Inn where the walk started.

# LEIGH

## WALK 5

★

6 miles (9.5 km)

OS Landranger 162, Pathfinder SO 82/92

Leigh is a small settlement 5 miles north of Gloucester and 4 miles south of Tewkesbury. It is reached by turning off the A38 1½ miles north of Norton. The scatter of houses are round a triangle of roads and are separated from the church. The start of the walk is on a lane which leads off the base of the triangle, next to the village pond. There are a number of wide verges along this lane. Please keep the gateways clear. (GR: SO 868 216)

Walk on down the lane which, after a gate, becomes a grass track. On reaching the very large field beyond, turn left and follow the path made by horses to a gate in the far right-hand corner. From here go between hedges and then bushes to a narrow bridge over the Coombe Hill Canal, long disused. This canal was built to take coal from the Severn to the nearest convenient point to Cheltenham, then a bustling new spa; had the fuel previously gone up Collier's Brook which was crossed earlier? The canal is only 2½ miles long and comes to a sudden end at the foot of the ridge, which is topped by the A38, at Coombe Hill, from where a narrow lane, cut deep in the rock, goes up from the old wharf to the main road to Cheltenham, only 5 miles away. As soon as the railway to Cheltenham was built, this canal went out of use.

Turn left along the tow path and at the road turn left. The second bridge you cross is over the river Chelt.

Wainlode Cliff, a few yards downstream from the Red Lion, is worth inspecting when the water is low. The base of the cliff is a bright red 'marl', while above it is a wide band of Tea Green Marl. On top of this are some bands of black shales and, in between, the famous White Bone Beds. Where the scree has been washed by the river it is easy to find 'fool's gold', which is actually pyrites but looks very much like real gold. Large crystals have been found, some as big as OXO cubes, but they can, of course, be easily distinguished from real gold by the shape of the crystals.

Opposite the Red Lion inn is an orchard with a stile in the bottom corner. Start the walk here and go up through the orchard. This is part

21

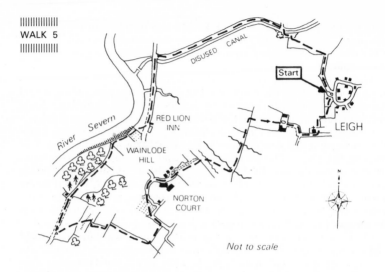

Start

Severn

River

RED LION
INN

WAINLODE
HILL

NORTON
COURT

LEIGH

DISUSED CANAL

N

*Not to scale*

of The Severn Way Walk and is waymarked. The path continues next to
the cliff on the right as far as a wood; take care that children do not run
too near the edge of the cliff. On reaching the wood leave The Severn
Way, which goes through the wood, and turn left up the field, keeping
near the edge of the wood, and at the stile at the top turn round and
admire the view. The tower of Leigh church stands out over to the right;
you will go through the churchyard later, to return behind the row of
trees in the valley.

From the stile go towards the highest part of the field, between two
woods. Continue through a gate at the end of the field. There is now a
track to follow as far as the concrete Ordnance Survey triangulation
pillar. Such pillars are often found on prominent hill tops and they form
a network over the whole of Britain, providing known positions and
heights from which local surveying can start. The pillars are sometimes
painted white so that they can be identified on aerial photographs.

From the OS pillar turn back to the left and following the grass track,
which goes to the left of a wood, aim towards Leigh church. As you cross
the field the tower of Norton Court comes into view ahead, ½ mile
away. In the middle of the next field go down the steep bank and bear
right, looking for a stile in the angle of the hedge. From the stile go down
the field with the hedge on the left. At the bottom turn left and in 20
yards turn right over another stile. Continue with the hedge on the left
for ¼ mile to a gate leading into the bottom of the field on the left, 100
yards from the end of the field you are in. Go through the gate and walk

with the hedge on the right out to the lane and turn left. In 100 yards, at the sharp bend, go straight ahead up into the corner of an orchard. Bear right to the far right-hand corner, crossing 8 ridges, to a gate on to the lane again.

Walk along the lane for 100 yards and turn right round a high garden wall. Continue past the clock tower of Norton Court on the right and Court Farm on the left to a gate into a field at the end of the lane. Keep this same direction over the hill ahead and then go down to a gate.

Cross the narrow field, then the farm bridge over Collier's Brook and then bear right to a new concrete bridge over the river Chelt. This river rises in the Cotswolds, 10 miles away, and flows under Cheltenham. After crossing the next bridge, over Leigh Brook, follow first the hedge and then the ditch on the right for ¼ mile into the second field where there is a small stone bridge on the right. When this is crossed, go up the field towards the left-hand side of the wide gap between the farm buildings. This will take you past a pond and along the farm drive.

Continue as far as the church. Go into the churchyard and pass to the right of the church. Bear right to a stile in the hedge and go into a field to walk with the hedge on the right. In 200 yards follow the hedge round to the right to a stile in the corner. In the next field turn left towards a fence near an angle in the hedge, 100 yards from the left-hand corner. Follow the hedge on the right in the next field to a gate which leads out on to the lane where the walk started.

# HASFIELD

## WALK 6

★

6 miles (9.5 km)

OS Landranger 162, Pathfinder SO 82/92

Hasfield is a small village which lies scattered along the hillside 5 miles north of Gloucester and 6 miles south-west of Tewkesbury on the west bank of the river Severn. It is reached from Gloucester by taking the A40 Ross-on-Wye road and in 1 mile turning right to Ledbury. In 3 miles turn right to Ashleworth and then follow the signs to Hasfield. From Tewkesbury take the A38 to Gloucester and in 3 miles turn right to Ledbury. In a further 4 miles turn left at Tirley at the first turning after Haw Bridge. From Cheltenham go towards Tewkesbury and in 6 miles turn left to Ledbury and Haw Bridge. On the road between Ashleworth and Tirley there are 3 turnings to Hasfield. Opposite the middle one there is an unsignposted lane. Turn down here. After ¾ mile, although the lane continues, it has not been tarmacadamed and is only suitable for tractors. It is a popular place for fishermen to park so, if there is room here, do so too; if not, the grass verges along the lane are sound. Do not park in front of, or opposite a gateway, as large slurry tankers may have difficulty in manoeuvring. The lane is busy as it serves a thousand acres of Hasfield Ham. (GR: SO 837 265)

Walk back along the lane towards Hasfield and, 200 yards before reaching the bend, you will see two gates almost opposite each other. Turn through the one on the right where there is a rough track and follow the hedge on the left to a farm bridge. In the next field keep the same direction to a small gap in the opposite hedge, 50 yards from the left-hand corner. Here cross the ditch into the corner of another field. Cross this field diagonally, aiming to the right of the distant farm buildings.

Go through a small plantation and in the next field bear right next to the hedge and then by a high brick wall. At the end of the high wall cross the fence in front and go forward a few yards to a gravel drive. If this is obstructed there is a gate out of the field to the left of the barn. Turn right and follow the drive round the end of a garden wall. Built into the end of the wall is a small room which is called a gazebo, where eighteenth century ladies would retire to watch the passing river traffic.

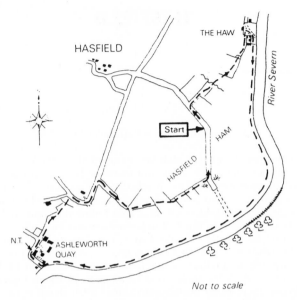

HASFIELD

THE HAW

River Severn

Start

HAM

HASFIELD

N.T. ASHLEWORTH QUAY

*Not to scale*

Continue walking along the bank of the river for 3 miles passing the cliffs of Wainlode on the other side of the river (see Walk 5).

Ashleworth Court, next to the church, was built about 1460 and has been altered less than most medieval buildings, though the roof was originally thatch. The footpath comes out at the end of a lane next to the Boat Inn which dates from the height of the river traffic, about 1830, when the industrial Midlands were expanding rapidly and railways had not taken away water traffic. In those days people thought of the main rivers and canals as today we think of motorways. Most rivers had a well-surfaced towing path. On the Severn the trows used sail whenever possible but often it was not. So the boats then had to be hauled, not by horses or donkeys as on other rivers, but by men, for there was a toll of 4d per mile for animals using the towpaths—and the men succeeded in resisting the change which would have meant loss of work. This 'bow-hauling' laid a great strain on them however, and many died of heart failure. A method employed, if the wind was contrary, was to use the incoming tide as long as it ran up river and then tie up and wait for the next tide. Consequently, every 3 or 4 miles along the river, there was a beer house and the Boat Inn is one which has changed little since those days. Before locks were built in the mid 1800s, a high tide could run up to Worcester.

As you walk up the lane you come to a large tithe barn where hay and grain were stored from the surrounding lands of the Abbey of St Augustine at Bristol. The abbey obtained the lands, so the story goes, from one Robert Fitzharding as an act of reparation because he eloped with a nun.

Continue past the front of the Court and, leaving the lane to go round to the left, go straight ahead into a field. Follow the hedge on the left round the large field to the far corner. Three quarters of the way round, pause to look over to the left at the large manor house which was built at about the same time as the tithe barn as a summer residence for the abbot. An extremely fine example of a large timber-framed building, it served for many years as a vicarage. From the corner walk on across a small field to the left-hand corner where you can see a white signpost at the road junction just beyond the gate.

Turn right along the lane for ½ mile to a stone track leading off to the right. Continue along here and in 200 yards go through the gate ahead. Walk on through the field to the gate opposite. From this point bear right for a few paces and then left along the near side of a hedge. Take care here as there is a ditch which may be hidden by the grass on this side of the hedge. In the corner go over a stile and cross the next field to a point 20 yards to the right of the gate opposite. This will take you along the side of a hedge to a gate in a corner. As you go across this field you can see a flood bank ¼ mile to your right for the river is just beyond, at the bottom of the wood. (You walked down there on your way to Ashleworth.) Continue next to the hedge and ditch on your left until you come to the rough track which is the continuation of the lane where the car is parked. Turn left back to the car.

You will notice that many of the fields at this end of the lane have two gates on to the lane, one nearer to Hasfield and one nearer the river. Until the last war, hay from these meadows was taken down to Hasfield Quay, which was then at the end of the lane but has now vanished, to be loaded on to boats for places such as Dudley Zoo and stables in Staffordshire. Each barge carried 12 tons up river and the return load was 32 tons of coal for sale locally. It was this sort of activity which made the river so busy in the past.

# PAUNTLEY

## WALK 7

★

4 miles (6.5 km)

OS Landranger 150, Pathfinder SO 62/72, 63/73

This walk climbs no great heights but the steep wooded slopes and open fields are typical of the Welsh border. Pauntley parish has a population of about 135 and in 1700 it was 115, so there has been little change for a long time.

Pauntley lies in the centre of a triangle formed by Gloucester, Ross-on-Wye and Malvern and it is 2 miles south of junction 2 on the M50. The walk starts from a country lane between Redmarley D'Abitot, a quiet village just off the A417, and Newent where it is sign-posted on the B4215 just outside the town. This rural lane goes down into a narrow valley, 2 miles from Newent and one from Redmarley, where it crosses the little river Leadon at Payford Bridge. Here there are a number of places to park the car, especially near the unsignposted side lane. (GR: SO 749 300)

The manor of Pauntley was one of 120 manors given to Walter de Laci by William the Conqueror. No doubt life went on much as usual except that an extra tax then had to be found for the overlord. In 1332 the manor passed by marriage to Sir William de Whittington. You will later come to the site of the manor house on a promontory overlooking the Leadon valley. Today a more recent house stands next to the church where lies buried Guy Whittington, High Sheriff of Gloucester, who died in 1427 (and, nearby, Charles Whittington who died in 1961). The fifteenth-century dovecote is all that is left of the birthplace of the most famous Whittington—Dick, or rather, Richard. Leaving aside legend, Richard went to London to learn the business of home and international trading and prospered greatly. After being Lord Mayor of London for 4 years (1406–7 and 1419–20) and contributing much to the rebuilding of London and Gloucester he died without heirs in 1423, leaving all his great wealth to charity.

Walk along the unsignposted lane in the valley. This lane rises up to go through Marrell's End Farm but on the way look over to the left where you can see Payford Mill with its great waterwheel. When the lane

27

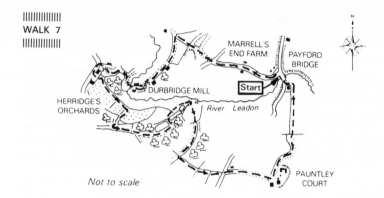

reaches a T-junction, go straight ahead through a gateway. In 200 yards, when the track sweeps round to the right, go straight ahead through a narrow cutting in the sandstone ridge and so down to a bridlegate. Now go straight across the next field next to a fence on the left and turn left along a stone track at the bottom of the field.

Walk along this track, passing first a cottage and then Durbridge Farm on the left, to go down the hill to Durbridge Mill. Go through the farmyard gate and follow the track round to the right and pass between the farm buildings; the end one on the right was the old mill. Just past the next gate bear right to an old bridge over the river Leadon. From the bridge follow the track out into the field and then to the right. At the end of the wood on the left turn left up a valley. Follow the edge of the wood for 100 yards and then turn left at the corner of the wood. In a further 100 yards bear right to climb up to the right of a flat platform where once stood some buildings. At the lane beyond the gate, turn left and in 200 yards turn left into the large entrance and store yard of Herridge's Orchards.

Keep straight ahead to a gate into the apple orchard and follow the left-hand boundary round the orchard. In ¼ mile pass the end of the second very tall, thin hedge dividing the orchard and acting as a windbreak. Turn right and walk with the hedge, or row of closely planted alder trees, on the right and when the trees end continue down to a stile in the boundary hedge on the right. Beyond is a sunken track which you follow and then go straight across the field in the valley. On reaching the opposite hedge near a gate, turn left and walk with the hedge on the right. Continue through the wood and at the end of the first lake turn left. After going through a gate in a fence, turn right to the end of a small clump of trees, where there is another gate.

In the field beyond, bear right towards an old footbridge but just

28

before reaching the bridge turn right to a gate in the fence. From here go straight up the field bearing slightly right. When you get over the brow of the hill you will see a gate ahead. There is a good track up the valley beyond the gate.

At the end of the wood on the left go through a gate and turn left up the field beside the wood. Continue through two fields, next to the hedge on the left, until you come out on to a lane at a T-junction. Cross and go down the lane signposted 'Pauntley Church and Court'. A simply-produced 12-page guide to the church of St John the Evangelist can be purchased for a small sum inside. It is a model for church and parish guides. Written anonymously in a clear style, it is divided into two parts, the second of which gives information on Dick Whittington.

Continue the walk by going down the track to the left of the manor house and in nearly ¼ mile go through the right of two gates. Follow the fence on the left which eventually becomes a garden hedge. When the hedge turns left, follow it to a gate on to the lane. Here turn right and in 100 yards cross the bridge back to the start of the walk.

# UPPER LODE

WALK 8

★

3 miles (5 km)

OS Landranger 150, Pathfinder SO 83/93

Upper and Lower Lode mark the two old crossing places on the river Severn near Tewkesbury. The river was unbridged until 1826 when Thomas Telford built his fine single span bridge at the foot of the Mythe Hill, just to the north of the town. At Upper Lode the Severn made a small loop and, until the improvements to navigation in the mid nineteenth century were undertaken, the larger barges and trows often had to wait a long time for flood or tide to carry them over the shallows. Before the railway age every merchant was resigned to having to wait an extra week or two in dry weather for his supplies. When it was realised that the railway could offer serious competition to water traffic, attempts were made to speed up the passage of larger vessels. Six weirs, with their attendant locks, were built at Gloucester, Tewkesbury, Worcester, Bevere, Holt and Stourport. This increased the depth of the river up to Bewdley, which was the highest large port on the Severn. At Upper Lode a bypass was cut across a loop in the river and a weir was made. The loop, which was called 'The Old River' on maps until recently, was closed off at one end, and is now gradually silting up.

The walk goes southwards along the higher ground, roughly following an old trackway above flood level, to return along the towing path.

Upper Lode is ¾ mile due west of Tewkesbury, on the west bank of the river. It is reached along a narrow 'No through road', which leaves the A438 road ½ mile from Telford's bridge. From Tewkesbury take the A38(T) towards Worcester and in ½ mile turn left towards Ledbury. A ¼ mile along the narrow lane, turn right at the entrance to the private road leading to the lock and park on the grass verge on the right. (GR: SO 880 332)

Walk on up the lane towards the hill in front. Follow the lane past the 2 remaining cottages of a once larger settlement of river folk and continue to a gate. Carry on along the field beyond, next to the hedge on the right. The unique view to the left across Tewkesbury Ham is at its best in late afternoon when the Abbey tower stands out against the distant Cotswolds. The yellow stone of the Abbey did not come from the

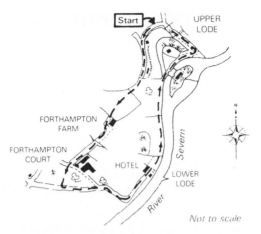

Not to scale

Cotswolds as might be expected but from Caen in Normany, for it was easier in the twelfth century to transport heavy loads long distances by water than even short distances by road.

Continue for 300 yards to go through a gate in a wire fence and then keep straight ahead towards the right-hand side of Forthampton Farm. Go round the farm buildings to the farm drive. The public right of way cuts across the corner of the ploughed field which was once grass parkland and joins the drive a little way from the farm. Turn right along the drive for ¼ mile. The high garden wall on the left—evoking pictures of a secret garden beyond—belongs to Forthampton Court. Walk on to the sharp right-hand bend at the entrance to the court and go straight ahead to a kissing gate. In the park beyond, go straight ahead passing just to the left of the tree a few yards from the gate, and cross to a small gate on to a fenced lane. Here turn left.

As you go along the lane there is a good view of Forthampton Court across the park to the left. It was here that the Abbot of Tewkesbury had a country house. The most important part of the medieval building still surviving is the Great Hall, built in about 1380. The huge bay window which lights the hall, and which was added in 1914, can be seen on the left.

Continue along the lane to the Lower Lode Hotel. Here was the lower, and more important, river crossing in pre-bridge days. Walk on along the river bank. In ½ mile you come opposite Lock Island, with its plantation of osiers, or persh as they are called hereabouts. The Middle English word persche for osier gives its name to Pershore. Cross the footbridge over Old Severn and walk past the lock.

The roadway takes you back to the start of the walk.

31

# TEWKESBURY

## WALK 9

★

5 miles (8 km)

OS Landranger 150, Pathfinder SO 83/93

The walk begins from the car park at the back of the old abbey church, now the parish church. Go down Gander Lane, which starts from the main road 200 yards towards the centre of the town from the abbey. It is well signposted. (GR: SO 894 326)

In times of flood Tewkesbury becomes an island, a peculiarity that prevented expansion after the Middle Ages. As the population increased they had to be accommodated in dwellings built at the back of the houses fronting the main streets. Most of the street houses are timber-framed, though many are now faced with Georgian brick. Access to the rows of cottages, mostly built in the seventeenth and eighteenth centuries, which fill the gardens, is by alleys. Mr Pickwick was made to stop and dine at the Hope Pole in Church Street and Mrs Dinah Craik's novel *John Halifax, Gentleman* was set in Tewkesbury. More recently, John Moore, in his *Portrait of Elmbury* and other novels, has given a nostalgic picture of the town.

Leave the car park and go into Recreation Park. Cross the lower part of the park, with the abbey on the right, to the far corner and out to the main road. Turn left uphill past the old toll house and in a few yards turn down Lincoln Green Lane. About 200 yards down the lane there is a notice on the right headed 'Bloody Meadows', an apt name for a battlefield. It was in 1471: the situation was that the Lancastrians were defeated at Barnet, just north of London. Margaret of Anjou and her son Prince Edward were delayed in the Channel by bad weather and landed a few hours too late for that battle, so they joined with Somerset and decided to go into Wales where Jasper Tudor was raising troops for the cause. Meanwhile Edward IV marched, with his usual speed, to stop them crossing the Severn. The Lancastrians first went to Gloucester but were turned away by the Yorkist townsfolk. They moved upstream and were about to cross at Tewkesbury when Edward caught up with them. Too late they turned and formed up across the valley in a line from behind where the new houses are today to what is now the golf course, over to the right. They were overcome and retreated, the few

32

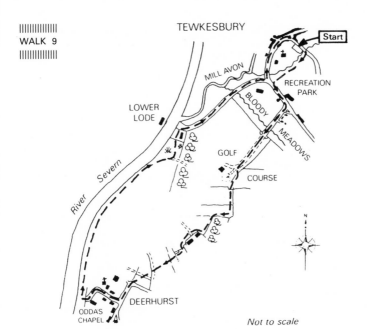

that were left, across the spot on which you are now standing. Indeed, so many Lancastrians were killed that the brook is said to have run red with blood.

Continue up the drive towards the golf course. (There is a fairway on the right and you are advised to walk up the left side of the drive!) The clubhouse was formerly a residence, built in the late eighteenth century but on the site of a fourteenth century house where Edward Despencer lived. When the main drive bears right, bear left down to a gap in the bottom hedge. There are yellow posts and waymarks to follow. Turn right below the hedge and cross two fairways to a stile leading to the corner of a field. Now follow the waymarked path through two fields to the right of the farm on the hill. Cross the farm track and pass the 'Ha Ha'. A Ha Ha is a sunken fence or wall to keep animals out of the garden without obstructing the view; thus, from the house, the lawn appears to stretch out to join the fields. A Ha Ha is said to get its name from what people used to say when they discovered why the animals did not come up to the house.

Follow the hedge and in 100 yards go round to a stile on the left and then turn right. In another 100 yards, at the top of the bank, look across

33

the fields to the group of houses well to the left of the church where there is a sharp bend in the road not far from a white signpost and make your way to this sharp bend by going down to a wide gap in the hedge below and following as straight a route as possible. Go along the road to the signpost and turn right. In 200 yards along this lane is the entrance to the church, which is well worth visiting. It dates back to the time of the Priory which was in existence in AD 804. Full information can be obtained inside the church. Then, 200 yards further along the road on the left, is Odda's Chapel which can be precisely dated to 12 April 1056. At one time the large timber-framed farmhouse was attached to one end of the chapel (not being recognised for what it was). The nave became the kitchen of the house while the chancel was divided into two floors. The chapel has been completely restored and is a good example of pre-Norman architecture.

The lane now becomes a track out to the river bank. Turn right upstream for 1½ miles. Go through an iron gate and cross in front of the boat house to the end of a lane. This is Lower Lode where there was an ancient river crossing. Continue along the lane next to the Mill Avon with the Severn Ham beyond. There was a racecourse here in the eighteenth century.

At the A38, opposite the gate into Recreation Park, turn left along the main road past the abbey. Just past the first building beyond the abbey entrance is a recently-restored row of timber-framed shops and houses. Lying outside the abbey precincts, these attractive buildings were put up by the monks to be let to tenants, probably as a speculative venture. They form also one of the oldest surviving examples of medieval town planning in the country.

At the end of the row turn right into Gander Lane.

# ALDERTON

## WALK 10

★

6 miles (9.5 km)

OS Landranger 150, Pathfinder SP 03/13

This walk climbs up over one of the small hills, which break up the lower Vale of Evesham, to visit a village with its hall and parkland on the other side—and returns over the hill again. Most of the land we walk upon today is part of a large estate, much of it devoted to pheasant rearing.

Alderton is a small village 7 miles south of Evesham and 7 miles east of Tewkesbury. It lies ½ mile north of the A438 Tewkesbury–Stow-on-the-Wold road and 2 miles south-east of the A435(T) Evesham–Cheltenham road and is signposted on both roads. If you approach from the A438 road, go into the village and, keeping to the main street, turn right twice; if you come into the village from the A435, keep the same direction through the village. Cars can be parked ½ mile out of the village on a road signposted to Toddington. This road turns into Dipden Lane and eventually goes out to the A438. (GR: SP 008 331)

Walk along Dipden Lane away from Alderton. At the sharp right-hand bend turn left on to a gated road. Follow the road round the house and go through a gate. Keep to the road for a further 100 yards, to a sharp right-hand bend. Here turn left on a faint grass track in the field for 100 yards. Turn right and go up the field to a gate near the corner of a wood. Follow the track up the hill, keeping near the edge of the wood. At the top of the first rise a track comes in from the right through a gate; here turn left across the head of the valley you have just come up. You will now go for almost a mile round the hill without any change of height.

Walk past a wood on the left and the head of a second valley, to a gate. Follow the track, with a wood now on the right, past the head of a third valley to cross-tracks. Go straight ahead and, a few yards inside the spinney, bear right towards a gate with a signpost to Dumbleton. (You will come back through here.) Do not go through the gate but turn left and walk through the spinney, having a hedge on the right.

Walk beside the hedge on the right for ½ mile although it is sometimes replaced by a fence where it has not been maintained. Eventually a grass track comes up the hillside and goes along near the

Not to scale

hedge. Follow this track down the hill. Just past the end of the field on the right, beyond the hedge, the track forks left and right and a grass track continues straight ahead. Go ahead along this track through a plantation of larches with elder bushes growing in their shade. At the bottom of the wood follow the track round to the right, just inside the wood. On reaching a gate in the hedge on the left, cross the stile at the side and stop and look over the fields. Down below you will see a farm and cottage; this is all that is left of a small medieval village which spread across into the field to the right of the buildings. From this point on the hillside you can also see the ridges and furrows made by the villagers, all of whom farmed in the same way. The ownership of land was in 'strips' or ridges and the number and position of these holdings, which were often scattered, denoted the prosperity of the farmer. The land was always ploughed in the same direction, the earth being thrown up to the right, and thus the ridges were formed. If a ploughman had worked the other way he would have filled up the furrow on either side, thereby extending his plot and gaining about 150 square yards of land. Consequently the ridges became very high and, if the land has remained pasture since the system ended at the time of enclosure, they can still be seen, though gradually they are being levelled out by natural forces.

Walk down the 'strips' and, 20 yards before reaching the gate into

36

Didcot Farm, turn right. Go along below a small bank, which was the headland of the 'strips', to a gate. From here go across a narrow uneven field (the deserted village) to a footbridge in the opposite hedge, 30 yards from the wood on the right. In the next field go up to the top right-hand corner and into the wood. Now turn left along a track just inside the wood with a hedge on the left. When the hedge ends, go through the gate in front and along the top edge of a field, next to the wood on the right. This is a very undulating path and opposite the middle of a small wood below on the left, go over a mount to bear right to a stile. There are two stiles here into a newly planted wood.

Go across the corner of this wood to another stile out into a field. Keep the same direction across this narrow field to a stile in a fence. As you approach the stile, look beyond it and note the direction to be taken to go straight ahead down the next large field. At the bottom of this field is an avenue of old trees which once flanked a driveway to Dumbleton Hall, seen away to the right.

From the stile in the fence keep the same direction to the middle of the fence which has a track and cricket field beyond. When you reach the track—the tradesmen's entrance—turn left and go out of the park on to the end of a roadway. Follow this past the red brick building, built in 1899, with an interesting plaque on the left of the entrance doors. At the T-junction turn right along the main street. Pass the ornate village water supply erected by 'Old friends of Edward Holland'. At the sharp left-hand bend bear right along a 'No through road' to Leyfield Farm.

Dumbleton Hall was built in 1830 in the Tudor style. It has an interesting porte-cochère (or covered porchway) into which carriages could drive but this is a later addition. The building is at present used as a recuperation centre for Post Office employees. In 200 yards, when the road forks, bear right and follow the bridleway sign to Alderton.

Follow the good road up to Hill Farm and, as you go up, you can admire the gardens of the Hall across the valley. On nearing the top of the hill, notice the ridges and furrows, which show to what lengths the villagers of Dumbleton once went to find land to plough in times of prosperity, for this must always have been marginal land, as it is today.

About 50 yards before reaching the farm, fork left round to a gate with a sign to Alderton. Follow the stone track to go through the gate with the Dumbleton sign which you saw on the way out, and walk back through the spinney. At the cross-tracks turn right and in 20 yards bear left down through the wood. At the end of the wood go through a gate into the corner of a field and follow the hedge on the left for ½ mile into Alderton. There is a stile to the right of the garden of the first house you meet, which leads to a narrow path. At the road in Alderton, turn left and walk out of the village towards Toddington.

Continue along Dipden Lane back to the start of the walk.

# LEDBURY

★

4 miles (6.5 km)

OS Landranger 149, 150, Pathfinder SO 63/73

This walk climbs the hills east of Ledbury and passes Eastnor Castle, to return through farmland to the main road south of the town. Ledbury is a fine example of a Herefordshire market town. It is, so far, unspoilt by the great number of visitors who come to see the fine timber-framed buildings and to get an idea of what Tudor and Stuart streets were like. The Malvern Hills District Council has produced an excellent and inexpensive illustrated guide and 'walkabout" to the town. It can be purchased at the Old Grammar School in Church Lane, the Information Centre or book shops—and because the guide is so good little has been said here about the town!

Situated at the crossing of the A499(T) Worcester–Ross-on-Wye road and the Hereford (A438)–Gloucester (A417) road, Ledbury lies 3 miles west of the Malvern Hills. It can also be reached on the A438 west from Tewkesbury. Cars may be parked in the two large car parks off Bye Street in the centre of the town, next to the clock tower. (GR: SO 711 377)

Walk out into Bye Street from whichever car park was used and go towards the centre of the town. On the corner of the street on the left is the Barrett Browning Institute, so named because the Barretts lived at Hope End, a country house 2 miles north of Ledbury, for several years before moving to Wimpole Street. Some ¼ mile up the street to the left is Knapp House, the birthplace of John Masefield who was Poet Laureate from 1930 to 1967. Cross the main street and go to the left of the seventeenth century Market House and up the narrow, cobbled Church Lane. This is one of the most photographed streets in the West Midlands and its few modern signs and street furniture are periodically unscrewed by film or television crews who are at work on a seventeenth or eighteenth century story. It is seldom free from amateur photographers from all parts of the world.

Continue into the churchyard and bear right. Notice that the church tower is detached from the main body of the church. Walk on through the churchyard and turn right along a wide path out to the Malvern

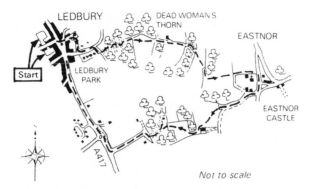

LEDBURY

DEAD WOMAN'S THORN

EASTNOR

Start

LEDBURY PARK

EASTNOR CASTLE

A417

*Not to scale*

Road, next to the police station, and turn left. In 200 yards cross the road with care and follow the sunken track beside the house called 'Conigree'. In 100 yards go through a gate into Conigree Wood, which is administered by the Forestry Commission.

Inside the wood take the left fork and follow the sunken track up the hill. Cross over two grass forest roads and continue for a further 200 yards to a small gate on the right which leads into a field on top of the hill. Go through here and in the field turn left. Aim along the side of the field towards a small round wooded hill, half a mile away. In the corner of the field go down on to a track through trees. Bear right and you soon come out into another field—actually it is all one big U-shaped field.

On the left is a derelict farmstead known as 'Dead Woman's Thorn'.

Walk on down the field, with the hedge on the left, to a gate and into the wood again. Follow the path through the wood and cross the small valley beyond, following the ridge across the field. This ridge is where the path has been left when the rest of the field was under plough—a practice much appreciated by walkers. Go through a gate and up the side of a hill. At the top turn left. Before going down another grass path, pause to look across Eastnor Park towards Midsummer Hill (Walk 12). Walk down the hill and in the next field keep near the hedge on the right, to go out on to a lane at the entrance to Eastnor Court. Turn right along the lane.

On the opposite side of the village green is the boundary wall of Eastnor Castle, the entrance to which is a little way down the lane to the left, opposite the picturesque post office, on a bend in the A438. The castle, which is open to the public at certain times, was built in 1812 in the Norman Revival style for the first Earl Somers. There is a real castle in the parish at Bronsil, begun in 1460 and now a ruin. It is in the valley below the obelisk in the park, not far from Midsummer Hill.

39

With the castle boundary wall on the left, leave the village green along a lane and in 50 yards bear right and go towards the estate offfice, which is the timber-framed building with brick nogging (infilling) across the field. Pass the farm and cottages and follow the track up to the left into the wood. In ¼ mile bear right down to a gate into a field. Over the hedge on the right notice a field full of black poplars. This crop—for trees are considered to be a long-term crop by farmers—is often planted on wet land, as the black poplar likes to have its feet in water. They are great drinkers, so much so that the surface dries up and then the land can be used for grazing.

From the gate, bear left up the valley (this is a bridleway) and, as you approach the top, bear right to a gate on the right of a farm. Pass the farm on your left and go towards a gate into a field in the next valley but do not go through the gate; turn right instead along a track at the end of the wood. In 50 yards go through a gateway into the corner of another field. From here the bridleway goes diagonally across the field to the far bottom corner but as there may be a crop planted it might be easier to go round to the right under the wood and so down to the corner.

At the time of writing, the wood beyond here is completely overgrown but should it be clear go into the wood and in 150 yards bear left along a grass track. If it is not clear, go along to the right near the hedge for 100 yards and enter the wood by a gate. About 20 yards inside the wood take the left track and in a further 100 yards fork left. The bridleway goes round the end of the hill and through a gate on to the end of a stone track. Follow this track down the hill to the main road and turn right.

Keep to the footpath which soon goes along beside the high park wall. On the left you will pass the entrance to a new housing estate with a road named Biddulph Way, after the Biddulph family who were lords of the manor for many years. Walk on into Ledbury. At the cross-roads the large house on the right is Ledbury Park where the Biddulphs lived for many years. Part of it dates from the sixteenth century but considerable additions were made in the seventeenth and nineteenth centuries.

Pass the Feathers Hotel on the left and return to the car park.

# MALVERN HILLS
# HOLLYBUSH

## WALK 12

★

6½ miles (10.5 km)

OS Landranger 150, Pathfinder SO 63/73

From Hollybush this walk climbs to the Hill Fort on Midsummer Hill and then turns southwards over the last two hills of the Malvern ridge.

The walk starts from the southern tip of Castlemorton Common, ½ mile east of the Hollybush pass, 4 miles from Ledbury and 10 miles from Tewkesbury, where the A438 goes over the Malvern Hills. Cars can be parked on the common near Hollybush church where the Malvern Hills Conservators have small green car park signs. Park at the western end of the unfenced common, nearest the hills. (GR: SO 767 368)

Walk away from the A438 road and go between a tiny black and white cottage on the right and a house built of Malvern stone on the left. A track will take you down to the left of a lake. Follow the hedge on the left for 50 yards past the lake and then turn left. In a few yards bear slightly right and then bear left in front of the first house on the left. Keep straight ahead along a narrow strip of common to bear right up to an unfenced road. Here turn left and in 200 yards fork left. It is here that many an intrepid aviator starts his hang-gliding career, climbing laboriously to the top of the hills on the right. A few—shortly afterwards—plunge ignominiously into the bracken half way down!

Keep to the lane for ¼ mile as it drops down to cross a stream and then to go along the hillside. On the right you will see a Conservators' car park—a large lay-by shaped area at the foot of the wood—at the beginning of which there is an opening into the wood. Go in here and turn left on the 'easy route' to the hill fort on the Midsummer and Hollybush Hills. This modern path will bring you into the southern end of the fortified camp. At the top turn right and walk along Hollybush Hill. You will now be walking northwards. The way out of the camp is by an original gateway at the northern end of Midsummer Hill to your left. First, however, you may like to explore this once densely populated encampment. There are, for example, over 200 hut sites on 11 small terraces on the east side of Midsummer Hill.

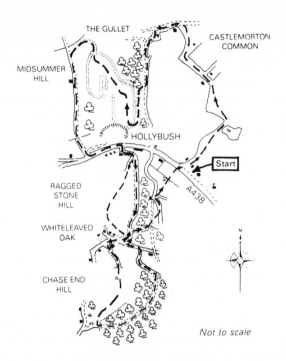

THE GULLET

CASTLEMORTON
COMMON

MIDSUMMER
HILL

HOLLYBUSH

Start

A438

RAGGED
STONE
HILL

WHITELEAVED
OAK

CHASE END
HILL

N

*Not to scale*

To continue the walk, go through the northern gateway and follow the path as it curves down to the left. Before you go down the path look over to the right into the quarry where you can clearly see how the slab of metamorphic rock has been pushed up to form the Malvern range. In the top left-hand corner of the quarry there are numerous layers of limestone exposed. These were laid down in the Silurian Sea 400 million years ago and have been pushed up so hard that they are folded back on themselves, like the rim of a bowl.

At the stone track turn left. From various places along this track there are excellent views. Below you in the valley are the ruins of Bronsil Castle (1460) hidden in the trees. Beyond is Eastnor Castle (1812) and in the far distance the Brecon Beacons with Hay Bluff at the right-hand end where the mountain suddenly ends.

Continue along the track to the main road (A438), cross it and turn left. In 200 yards you will find an old turnpike milestone now almost buried in the pavement. Turn right opposite the entrance to a disused quarry and go up a track to the left of the post office. Just past the gate on to the hills the energetic can turn right and go over the top of the

Ragged Stone Hill. They should then keep the same direction down to a small settlement called Whiteleaved Oak. The easier route is on the track along the side of the hill to Whiteleaved Oak. In the nineteenth century romantic novel *The Shadow of the Ragged Stone*, a monk of Little Malvern Priory fell in love with the daughter of a local knight and was given a penance by the Abbot. The poor fellow was ordered to go up the Ragged Stone Hill twice a day on his knees. After some weeks of this he could take it no more and, before expiring, laid a curse on all those upon whom the shadow of the Ragged Stone fell. *If you are walking in the afternoon you will have been in the shadow of the Ragged Stone!*

When you get to the lane keep ahead going round to the left. Look for a gatepost on the right; the other post and the gate have lately disappeared. It is here that the three counties of Hereford (to the right), Gloucester (in front) and Worcester (to the left) meet, though for administrative purposes Hereford and Worcester are now one. At this point turn left and follow a hedged track towards the top of Chase End Hill.

Having rested and admired the views, keep to the previous direction down the hillside to a hedge where there is a cross-track. Turn left here and follow a good track through the wood for ¾ mile. At the lane turn left and in 200 yards turn right up a track—if you did not go over the top of the Ragged Stone you will have come out this way.

In 200 yards the path dips down near a small spring. As the path starts to rise up again look on the right for another one down through the wood. Follow this path to a gate into a field. From here the right-of-way bears right to cross a stone track to a stile in the hedge bordering a sunken road. The walk continues by turning left along the lane as far as a lodge. At the time of writing, there is a wire fence at the side of the stone track and the stile is obstructed but if this is clear, follow the description above. If not, turn left along the track (which is a disused entrance to Bromsberrow Place) and leave the field by the wooden gate next to the lodge. The stone track is often used by walkers but is not a right-of-way.

Opposite the lodge—which sould be noted as a piece of architectural virtuosity—go over a stile to the left of the start of a hedged track. In the field beyond, aim at a point 100 yards to the right of the black and white house seen in the distance across the second field. Negotiate the intervening hedge near a small pond and keep the same direction to a stile in the roadside hedge. This will bring you to within 50 yards of the starting place.

# UPTON UPON SEVERN
# HOLDFAST

WALK 13

★

5 miles (8 km)

OS Landranger 150, Pathfinder SO 83/93, 84/94

Upton is 10 miles south of Worcester, 7 miles north of Tewkesbury and 8 miles west of Pershore. From the M5, turn on to the M50 (Ross Spur) and leave it at the first exit point. Follow the signs to Worcester and in 4 miles turn left.

The two Walks 13 and 14 start from the large car park near the river bridge, next to the Regal Garage. One walk goes south, the other crosses the river and goes north. Both return along the river bank. (GR: SO 850 408)

The town of Upton grew as the traffic on the river prospered. It began as a ton or settlement 'up' from Ripple, which is now only a small village and dwarfed by its original satellite. An ancient river crossing was here, but it had a bridge by the sixteenth century, if not before. It once had considerable wharves and, as most tides reached up as far as Upton, it was the furthest point inland to which some traders operated. The town acted as the port for Herefordshire and Monmouthshire. Below Upton the larger vessels could work more easily, some going round the coast to London—because of the state of the roads, it was easier to go 700 miles by water than 100 by land.

The largest boat on the river was the trow. Trows ranged from 25 to 120 tons weight and had a main and top mast of about 80 feet.

Go to the back of the car park in Upton upon Severn and leave by a short footpath. At the lane turn left and in 100 yards pass a plaque set into a stone pillar on the right which tells us that it was here that Goom Stool Cottages stood, named after the ducking stool. The origin of the word 'goom' is obscure. It may have come from the Welsh Border word 'gome' meaning 'greasy mixture'—and seventeenth century records show the water was exceedingly foul here—or from the Anglo-Saxon 'gumstol' (mockingly, a great person).

Continue for a few yards and turn right and go into the playing field. Keep to the right-hand side, past the end of an embankment, the

44

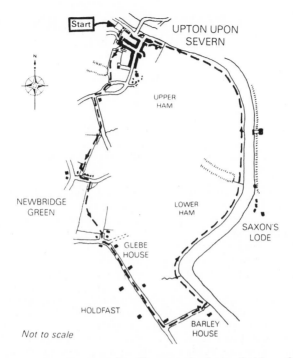

remains of an old railway and walk on to the loop of old road. Turn right and on reaching the main road go right and in 50 yards cross, with care, to the beginning of a long disused drive, next to the lodge. As you approach the first bridge, look on the right for a stile which leads in a few yards to the corner of the field. Go into the next field and follow the hollow-way on the left.

Pass through a riding school and along a lane to a T-junction at Newbridge Green. Turn left and a few yards before the lane bears left go over a stile on the right, next to a small, triangular clump of trees. In 20 yards go over a second stile. Now follow the hedge on the right for 150 yards to a gateway in this hedge. From here turn left towards the far corner of the field, just to the right of a small village hall. It sometimes seems a little strange to have to follow a circuitous route across an open pasture but the public rights of way, which entitle us to walk on other people's property, still follow the route laid down many years ago and can only be altered by due legal process. Go out of the field by the gate and so to the lane.

Turn left and follow the lane round to the right. On the bend you pass

45

the entrance to Ham Court. This old estate was broken up in the early part of this century, after more than 1,100 years. The Glebe House, just past the bend, is partly sixteenth century, with an interesting example of herring-bone brick nogging (brick infill). Continue along the lane past Holdfast Post on the left and in a further ½ mile turn left along a track. This leads past a small timber-framed cottage called the Barley House. The name, which is mentioned in the Domesday Book as Burgelege, comes from the Old English 'burh' or stronghold and 'leah' a clearing. Was there a fort here, on the high ground overlooking the river, defending a large settlement and clearing further to the west?

Go through the field gate and on down to the river bank. Turn left and follow the river for two miles. The great fields between here and Upton are called Hams. An Old English word hamm, which in its Middle English spelling is often ham, is easily confused with the more common ham, a farm or estate or, later, a manor. This ham means low-lying pasture or land near a river. (Place names are not always what they seem to be!) In ¾ mile the houses on the opposite bank form a settlement called Saxon's Lode and just beyond is a wartime underground petrol depot, which was fed by the last of the Severn tankers. A little further on is the inlet for the Coventry water supply.

At the end of the Ham go along the waterfront. The third house, seen through the wrought iron gates, is the Malt House and the building on the left of it is the King's Stable, where the Tudors and Stuarts kept a stable of horses. At the Swan Hotel, fork left along Dunns Lane to the site of the Old Church. Set in the graveyard wall opposite the Star Hotel are flood marks but unfortunately the highest flood in 1947 is not recorded although it came up to the window sills of the Star Hotel.

Continue past the Old Church, scene of the Battle of Upton in 1651 when a small detachment of Roundheads defeated a superior force of Royalists, thereby preventing the King using the Upton road for reinforcements to the imminent Battle of Worcester.

Walk on past 'Cromwells', one of the oldest buildings in the town, and so to the car park.

# UPTON UPON SEVERN
# RYALL'S COURT

WALK 14

★

3 miles (5 km)

OS Landranger 150, Pathfinder SO 84/94

The start for this walk is the same as for Walk 13, the large car park near the river bridge next to the Regal Garage at Upton. (GR: SO 850 408)

From the car park cross the river bridge and in 50 yards go down a sloping path on the left, following the footpath sign to Earls Croome. From the stile bear left across the meadow to a gate in the far hedge about 200 yards from the right-hand corner. In the next field keep the same direction to cross a fence to the right of a brush-jump, which is a part of the point-to-point course. Now bear slightly right towards the right-hand end of the farm buildings seen ahead.

After crossing the brook by the wide, grassed-over farm bridge, go to the corner of the field, just to the right of the next jump. Here the footpath should go over the ditch to the right of the gate but at the time of writing there is no bridge. However, go through the gate and bear right to the stone track which runs along just below the hill. Turn left along the track, passing in front of Ryall's Court Farm, and continue for ½ mile.

On reaching the second cattle-grid, turn left through a gate into a field and then turn right next to the hedge on the right. The house in the orchard used to be two cottages, known as Dayhouse Cottages. The nearest habitation is at least ½ mile away and it is food for thought that people still go to great lengths to live in isolation, as did the hermits of old. Continue with the hedge on the right to the river.

At the end of the wood on the cliffs overlooking the river, four bridleways and one footpath meet. There was here a small wharf where farm produce from the land to the east of the river was shipped to the cities and necessities, such as coal, were brought in. Being on the outside of the bend in the river the bank here has been considerably eroded. Within the past 100 years there was a towing-path along beneath this wood and in Tudor times the river would have been 20 or 30 yards further away.

47

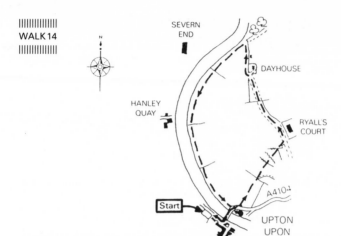

||||||||||||||
**WALK 14**
||||||||||||||

SEVERN END

DAYHOUSE

HANLEY QUAY

RYALL'S COURT

A4104

Start

UPTON UPON SEVERN

*Not to scale*

Turn left and follow the river bank. The building seen away across the river is Severn End, the seat of the Lechmeres, parts of which date back to the mid-seventeenth century. The next group of buildings, stretching down to the riverside, are at the old Hanley Quay and the large warehouse is all that is left of a once busy riverside settlement.

Continue to a gate under the road, 50 yards to the left of the bridge. Pass under the road and in a few yards turn back to the right, up to the road. Turn left. The red sandstone tower of the old church, with its copper-sheathed cupola, is called 'The Pepperpot' and is a landmark of which the town is exceedingly proud. The row of houses opposite the bridge, with Queen Anne fronts, was once the Manor House.

Turn right back to the car.

# BREDON HILL
# ASHTON-UNDER-HILL

## WALK 15

★

7½ miles (12 km)

OS Landranger 150, Pathfinder SO 83/93

Ashton-under-Hill is 4 miles south of Evesham. It lies ½ mile west of the A435(T) road between Evesham and Cheltenham, from which it is well signposted. Cars can be parked in the main street, at the upper end where it widens out to twice its usual width. (GR: SO 997 382)

Bredon is an outlier of the Cotswolds, of which it once formed a part. It measures some 3 miles by 1½ miles and rises to almost 1,000 feet, dominating the Severn Valley and the Vale of Evesham. From its heights there are magnificent views to the Birmingham uplands to the north, along almost the entire scarp face of the Cotswolds to the east and over the Malverns to the mountains of Wales to the west.

This walk at the eastern end goes round the lower slopes, through the picturesque villages of Grafton, Conderton and Overbury, to climb through Overbury Park and return with fine views over Evesham to Stratford-upon-Avon.

The past of Ashton 'Undrill'—as it is pronounced—has been brought to life by Fred Archer in his books on Bredon, for Ashton was his village, and many of the places he mentions are visited on this walk.

Walk down the main street and turn right opposite the T-junction to go into the churchyard through the kissing gate on the left of the lych gate. Walk up the path to the left of the church to leave the churchyard by a gate. At the end of a short narrow path, with a pond on the left, turn left by the side of the fence bordering the pond. Continue to a gate and in the next field bear right to the far corner of the field, just below a house. This small settlement is called Paris.

Go out on to a track along the side of the hill. Keep the same direction to a footbridge and a path which has been left unploughed across a field. At the lane, with its duplicated footpath signs, keep straight ahead to Middle Farm. This is within the settlement called Grafton, where there is an Upper, Middle and Lower Farm and a handful of cottages, almost unaltered since before the time of enclosure in 1773. Its parent village of Beckford lost its farms when the ownership of land was 'rationalised'.

49

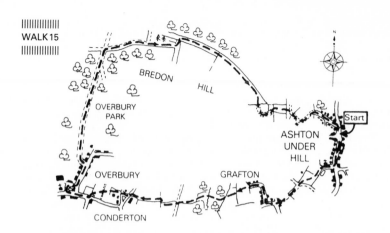

BREDON HILL

OVERBURY PARK

OVERBURY

ASHTON UNDER HILL

GRAFTON

CONDERTON

Start

Turn right up the hill, passing the village's former water supply on the left in 100 yards; thankfully, it is now replaced by piped water to each house. At the end of the lane bear left down to a gate. Go straight ahead into the field to the top of the rise in front. From here aim for a stile in the distant hedge which is level with where you are standing, about 300 yards up from the bottom left-hand corner. Keep straight ahead in the next field to a stile into the wood, 100 yards from the end of the wood. As you go across this field you can see, ½ mile down to the left, ponds left by gravel extraction. A few years ago archaeologists mounted a large excavation here and found evidence of man's continued settlement from the Bronze Age to Roman Times. Here, as in so many other places in the country, our ancient monuments below ground are being completely destroyed—for ever.

Continue through the wood and over the ride beyond. Cross the narrow stream and go through a small stand of black poplars. In the large field, walk next to the fence and then the hedge on the left, to the corner. Cross the track, but now continue with the hedge on the right. Go down to the corner of the second field and turn right. In the next field turn left round the edge. 100 yards up from the corner, look on the left for a small footbridge and hunting gate. Beyond here follow the hedge on the left for ½ mile out to a lane and turn left. This is Conderton and the house on the left is the old Manor House.

In 100 yards, at the end of the lane, is one of the oldest pubs in the area. Turn right opposite the entrance to the Manor House and as you go along you will see ahead a stone stile into an orchard. This is the beginning of the path to Overbury. Go straight across the orchard, over a stile and in a few yards through a gate and across the field to a stile opposite. Cross the narrow strip of rough ground and in the next field go to the opposite side just to the right of the garden of a small house. Climb the fence into a playing field and turn left to the road—where you will discover that the small house was once a toll house. The roadway has been made up so many times over the past 100 years that it is fast approaching the window sills. Opposite is the Star Inn, placed discreetly a little distance out of the village and away from the 'Great House'. Turn right along the road.

Overbury is an example of an estate-planned village. There must have been a great upheaval in the early eighteenth century when the Court was built and its extensive outbuildings and park laid out. During the last 100 years the village has been 'beautified' and the first example you will see of this is the village store on the left as you enter the village. Walk on to the tiny village-pond on the right—which would be an asset to any garden—and turn right. Just past the church is the entrance to the Court and you will note the retainers' houses on the road to the right. Go past these and at the T-junction turn left up the hill. In ¼ mile turn left through the imposing entrance to the park and follow the private road up through the park for 1 mile. This is a bridleway.

On emerging from a wood at the top of the park, turn right so as to have a wall and narrow belt of trees on the right. When this roadway turns left up to a transmitting station, go straight ahead. In ¼ mile, at a T-junction of grass tracks, turn left and go through two gates to a cross-track next to a wood. Turn right and follow the edge of the plateau for 1 mile until you come to the corner of a field with a fence in front. The gate, a few yards to the right in the fence, is the start of a track down to Ashton.

Go down and round to the left. Do not follow the 'Wyvern Way' signs, which would take you round to the church, but go through a gate and on round for nearly 100 yards. Now bear right downhill, keeping the hedge 20 yards away to your left. From the gate at the bottom of the field follow the track down to the right. Continue along this track, which soon improves and eventually becomes a lane, down into Ashton and the start of the walk.

# BREDON HILL
# LITTLE COMBERTON

WALK 16

★

8 miles (13 km)

OS Landranger 150, Pathfinder SO 84/94

To reach the start of this walk, leave the A44 at Pershore Bridge, on the outskirts of the town. The turning is signposted to the Combertons of which there are two, one Great and one Little. Follow the signs to Little Comberton and go through the village. A ¼ mile past the church, which is at the far end of the village, a wide hedged track, signposted 'Bridleway', on the right goes towards the hill. The walk starts here. (GR: SO 790 424)

Bredon is an outlier of the Cotswolds, of which it once formed a part. It measures some 3 miles by 1½ miles and rises to almost 1,000 feet, dominating the Severn Valley and the Vale of Evesham. From its heights there are magnificent views to the Birmingham uplands to the north, along almost the entire scarp face of the Cotswolds to the east and over the Malverns to the mountains of Wales to the west.

This walk climbs up to go round the western edge where the Severn and Avon valleys can be seen laid out below.

Walk along the bridleway which eventually climbs up steeply through a wood. On reaching the plateau at the end of the wood, cross the field and continue up a track for ¼ mile to a wood where another track comes up from the left. On the way back you will come down to this point from the right but now you go through the right-hand gate into the wood. Emerging from the wood at the top, go straight across to a small gate in the fence and climb up the field beyond, aiming slightly to the left of the tree-tops which can just be seen on the skyline.

Pass the trees, which surround an old quarry, and keep straight ahead to a gate. In the next field follow the fence on the right down to Lalu Farm and then go through two gates to a tarred farm road. Walk on downhill and at the beginning of a wood turn right along a track, with a wall and narrow belt of trees on the left. In 200 yards turn left down another track. Follow this track for ½ mile and after going through a small wood, continue down a lane.

The first building on the right is Bell's Castle and is a more pleasing

52

folly than most. The boy amongst the figures on the end wall of the garden is holding a bowl of fruit, not operating a video camera, as you might think! In a further ½ mile, after passing the Priory and the first turn on the right, go along the second lane on the right as far as the T-junction. This is the upper end of Kemerton village and the walk will continue to the right, but should you wish to explore the village, with its picturesque houses and old-world coaching inn, turn left—but return to this point.

53

Walk on up the lane and at the sharp right-hand turn go ahead up the stone track. At the top of the second field on the left, turn left on a well-worn path along the edge of the field. The right of way formerly went across the middle of this field but since the war, when these fields were turned from pasture to arable, people have always come this way. Follow the track past the cottage and at the stone track turn right. When the track forks, bear left and go on climbing up the hill.

At the first gate turn left and at the corner turn right. On the left below the path are some oddly shaped stones, rising some 15 feet out of the hillside. They are known as the King and Queen Stones. The Court Leet used to meet here until just over a hundred years ago, and on these occasions the stones were carefully whitewashed. To geologists, however, they are 'gulls', formed as follows. As the steep limestone hillside slowly slips and dissolves away, cracks are made in the hard surface rock. These cracks fill with small stones and limewater, forming 'nature's concrete'. As the hillside continues to erode, the pillars are left standing.

Continue with the fence on the right and go round an old walled quarry. The wall continues past a wood and in the corner of the second field there is a hunting gate. This leads to a wide track with a belt of trees on the left. Follow this for ¼ mile to go through a field and up to a squat tower which has lately sprung a number of antennae—something to do with 'car phones'. The tower is called Parson's Folly and was built in the late eighteenth century by Mr Parson of Kemerton Court. It increases the height of the hill to 1,000 feet!

You are now inside an Iron Age camp. As you will see there was little need for fortifications on the scarp sides but where the camp faced level ground there are two massive ditches. Two thousand years ago they would have been much more impressive, with vertical stone faces and topped by a palisade. The lower ground west of the Cotswolds supported a considerable population, for not everybody lived in a camp and over a dozen similar camps can be seen from various places on Bredon. Occupation here came to a sudden and violent end early in the first century AD; the mutilated bodies of over 50 defenders were found in the ditch near the entrance.

Continue round the hill, going through a small gate out of the camp field. At the end of the next field the gate leads to a track beside a wood. From the end of the wood, follow the fence on the right for 100 yards and then bear slightly left to follow a faint grass track which goes down the side of the hill to the bottom corner of an old wood.

Earlier in the day you came up the track from the left, so now turn left and retrace your steps to the car.

# MALVERN HILLS
# UPPER WYCHE

## WALK 17

★

3½ miles (5.5 km)

OS Landranger 150, Pathfinder SO 64/74

By geologists this walk may be called the 'Silurian Walk', for it goes over the pushed-up edges of the layers laid down at the bottom of the Silurian Sea some 400 million years ago. It also shows how different rocks affect scenery. The walk starts high on the Malvern Hills and climbs to the top of one of the hills, from which there is a magnificent view of the surrounding country. From these hills Piers the Plowman looked down on '. . . A faire felde ful of folke . . .' and Elgar received much of his inspiration.

This unique line of hills is made up of some of the oldest rocks in Britain. They are thought to have originally been shales or sandstones but about 600 million years ago they were crystallised and then pushed up in two separate thrusts, the latest one only 270 million years ago!

The walk then goes down over alternate layers of limestone and shales, each with its own characteristic scenery.

The Malvern Hills have many small car parks provided by the Hills Conservators—one of the first conservation bodies dating back to 1884. On the west side of the hills, between the Wyche cutting and the Herefordshire Beacon, is an unfenced road called the Jubilee Drive and half way along it is a small disused quarry, now a car park, opposite 'The Kettle Sings' café. The walk starts from here. Should the quarry be full of cars there is ample space nearby. (GR: SO 766 421)

Standing at the entrance to the quarry and looking out over Herefordshire, turn right along the grass above the road. In 50 yards join the wide track going up the side of the hill. At the top bear left on a path, which is almost level, along the top edge of a wood. The more energetic, however, can go over the top of the small hill on the right of the path. At the end of the wood go straight ahead to the top of the next hill (1,000 ft).

Continue along the hill to the Wyche cutting. As you cross the road going towards West Malvern you are on the Upper Llandovery Series which, though the highest, was the first to be laid down. 150 yards along

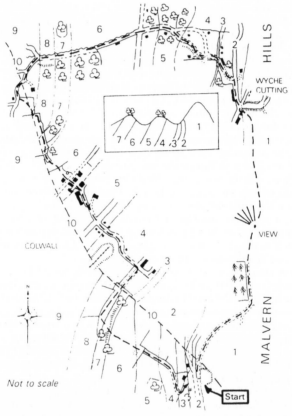

*Not to scale*

1 Malvernian
2 Mayhill Sandstone or Wyche Beds
3 Woolhope Limestone
4 Wenlock Shales
5 Wenlock Limestone

6 Lower Ludlow Beds
7 Aymestry Limestone
8 Upper Ludlow Beds
9 Devonian — O.R.S.
10 Fault line

this road look on the left for a track which runs steeply down the hill and is called 'The Purlieu'. Go down here and in 200 yards, opposite the third house on the right, the track levels out and goes over a small ridge which is, in fact, a narrow belt of Woolhope Limestone.

Now the track dips steeply down again, this time over the softer Wenlock Shales. At the first sharp right-hand bend go ahead down a grass path. Just before reaching the stone track again you will be on Wenlock Limestone. This makes up the higher part of the wooded hill on your right as you go on down the track. When a cross-track comes into view 50 yards ahead, look in the bank on the right for the change from blue-grey Wenlock Limestone to the more yellow Lower Ludlow Shales. The walk will cross straight over the wide stone track.

Many houses in Malvern are built of Malvernian rock, as seen in the quarry car park. Having no bedding plane it will not split into rectangular blocks (though the colours are very attractive when first quarried) and it therefore requires vast quantities of mortar when a wall is built. Until this century, lime was used where we now use cement. About 50 yards up the wide stone track to the right are the remains of an old lime kiln in which Wenlock Limestone was processed.

Walk down the narrow path, which may be muddy in places, to the better path next to the wood on the left. This wood and the one across the field on the right are both on hills where the Aymestry Limestone comes up. Further on the Upper Ludlow Beds are again softer. They can be seen clearly in the quarry face on the left, just before the end of the wood. On reaching the road the Devonian Old Red Sandstone stretches out before you for 40 miles.

Turn left along the road. Pass the entrance to Brockhill Farm on the left and in just over 100 yards, opposite the lodge on the right, look for a stile in the hedge on the left. Go diagonally across the field beyond to the opposite corner where there is a gate. In the next field turn left round the edge to go beside a tree-covered bank down to a stile at the end of the narrow neck of field. From here bear slightly left across to a stile.

Beyond the stile the footpath goes over the corner of playing fields just to the left of a new classroom block of the Downs School where, as you can see, they are keen on model railways.

Cross the wide stone track and go to the right of a short row of conifers and up between various outbuildings. In 50 yards, when confronted with a hedge, turn right and follow the hedge on the left past the back of the school buildings, to a stile. Keep the same direction down the drive beyond to the main road.

Cross the road with care and go along Broadwood Drive, opposite; when the drive sweeps round to the right the entrance to a railway tunnel under the hills is down on the right. When you go along the next straight length of drive you will observe, ahead, a gate into a field and a concrete stile on the left which is unique. How somebody must have enjoyed making it!

Go along the track in the field, passing four walnut trees on the right. Further away to the right, just beyond the railway, is the Schweppes factory where Malvern Water is bottled. It comes from a spring, deep in the hillside of the Herefordshire Beacon, a mile away in front of you, and is piped into the factory. Beyond the next gate the footpath bears right so as to follow the hedge on the right for 200 yards to where there is a stile on the right. Here turn left and start the ascent back to the quarry where the walk started.

Bear slightly right up the bank from the stile to go up through the trees. Keep this direction for 20 yards in the next field and then go straight up and over the field to a fence at the end of a hedged grass track. This fence is near a great pile of rubble which was once a barn. Go up the track and in 100 yards follow it up to the right. The building you can see high up on the left is 'The Kettle Sings' café and the stile is in the hedge 100 yards to the right of it.

Beyond the stile turn left and opposite the café turn right up to the quarry.

# EVESHAM

## WALK 18

★

5 miles (8 km)

OS Landranger 150, Pathfinder SP 04/14

This walk goes through some of the many hundreds of acres of orchards which surround Evesham. The wonderful sight and smell of these in blossom-time can only be appreciated to the full by the walker.

The market town of Evesham has pleasant lawns and tree-lined walks along the banks of the Avon. A Benedictine Abbey, founded in 714, added importance to the little community, called Ethom, who lived in this well-defended loop in the river. It was near here in 1265 that Simon de Montfort was defeated by Henry III's son, Edward, after a terrible battle when more than 4,000 fell on the hill to the north of the town. Today Evesham is the centre for both commercial and cultural activities in south-east Worcestershire.

The walk starts from the large car park near the fire station, on the opposite side of the A435 Cheltenham road to the museum and the Abbey remains. (GR: SP 035 437)

Go to the front of the fire station and cross to the far right-hand corner where a lane is signposted to 'Hampton Ferry ¼ mile'. At the ferry you may have to wait a few minutes for the ferryman to arrive for he is kept quite busy, since the ferry saves the people in the housing estates across the river an extra mile's walk into Evesham. Read the notice at the waterside to make sure the ferry will still be operating when you return in 3 hours.

At present there are a few months during winter when the ferry only operates at weekends. If this is so turn left and walk along by the river to the road bridge and back along the other side to a small road bridge over the little river Isbourne. Here turn right into a field and go to the side of the Avon and follow the path to the ferryman's cottage.

Go under the old railway bridge behind the ferryman's cottage, keep ahead into the field and walk up the hill to the top left-hand corner and beyond follow a hedged footpath out to a lane. Turn right up the hill. The lane soon turns into an unfenced track through orchards of plum and apple. When a gap in the trees in the right occurs there is a good view across the valley to the hill north of Evesham where the famous

59

CHARLTON

RYDEN

RYDEN FARM

YESSELL FARM

Avon

River

EVESHAM

Start

HAMPTON

FERRY

1265

*Not to scale*

battle took place. After ½ mile go straight over the cross-track and in a further ¼ mile pass a modernised farm on the right. Keep the same direction on a well used path and then a lane for 1 mile.

Away to the right is Ryden Farm. Here is a typical example of the way a name changes over the years. The farm was called Ridon earlier this century, Rowden House in 1830 and through various changes from Rudun (Rye hill) in 1220. At the next house on the right it is sometimes possible to see the mountains of Wales immediately in front.

Continue into Charlton (Ceorletum in 780—a settlement of freemen). At the main road through the village turn left, pass one of Worcestershire's many black and white post offices on the right and walk up the hill and along the straight road. In ½ mile, at the sharp left-hand bend, go straight ahead along a concrete drive next to the farm. (The footpath sign has usually been turned round to point to the bridleway which is on the right.) Enter the caravan park and keep straight ahead to the T-junction. Look ahead for a stile between caravan plots.

Continue ahead to a second stile and then keep the same direction through the orchard. After about 100 yards, go to the left of the huts used for storing boxes. Cross the next strip of land with a house and

60

buildings away to the left. Immediately after the next stile turn left over another stile to go down the side of a square field to the lane from Charlton.

Cross the lane and go down the track opposite. In 200 yards pass through the gap in the hedge and turn right beside the hedge. After 100 yards the footpath bears left across the field to the left of a giant pylon. There is a footbridge over the stream just behind the second wooden electricity pole. Cross the stream and keep the same direction on a track up the hill to a gate. Immediately beyond turn left through another gate and follow the hedge on the right down to a stile. Keep the same direction for ½ mile, following the hedge on the right through orchards until you come to a wide track.

Turn right down the track—you came along here on the way out. In 100 yards go to the left along the hedged footpath and so to the top of the field overlooking Evesham.

Go down the hill to the ferry. If the ferry is not working, turn right and retrace your steps over the road bridge.

# SOUTH LITTLETON

## WALK 19

★

6 miles (9.5 km)

OS Landranger 150, Pathfinder SP 04/14

The three Littletons—North, Middle and South—are sheltered on the west by slightly higher ground and away to the east by the Cotswolds. The Littletons lie in one of the most important market garden districts in 'The Vale' and this walk goes through some of the market gardens, with their crops of rhubarb and thyme, onions and asparagus (known locally as 'gras'). It is a strange world of men and women bent double, weeding, or sitting in rough shelters preparing crops for market. Many of the smallholdings are still run as family concerns. In the 1930s there were some 3,000 of these small units of between 3 and 15 acres round Evesham and the same around Pershore. The breaking up of the large estates in the nineteenth century was greatly encouraged by the acceptance of the 'Evesham Custom', whereby tenants owned the improvements made to their holdings and could realise the added value as 'ingoing' paid by the new tenant. Life in 'The Vale' is almost in another world, now fast disappearing, of hard work for little return save the freedom of working the land for oneself and of being one's own boss in the open air.

The walk starts from South Littleton, which is on the B4085 Bidford-on-Avon–Badsey road, 1½ miles north-east of Evesham. It is reached from the A439(T) at Bidford by crossing the Avon and following the signs through Cleeve Prior, or from Evesham by taking the B4035 towards Weston Subedge and turning on to the B4085 near the 'Round of Gras'. Cars can be parked on a short elbow-shaped road, which was the original main road before straightening and widening took place. It is 100 yards north of the church. (GR: SP 076 463).

In the corner of the elbow is a footpath sign. Go along the footpath between the houses and round to a kissing gate and in the field beyond turn left. The ridges and furrows in this field are a relic of the pre-enclosure days when life was very different because most people were farmers. In the sixteenth century the Vicar of Badsey, just down the road, was responsible for the parish bull but in South Littleton he was only responsible for the parish 'heyfur'.

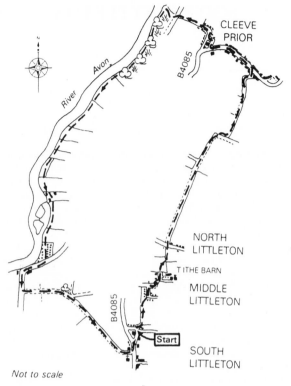

CLEEVE
PRIOR

River Avon

B4085

NORTH
LITTLETON

TITHE BARN

MIDDLE
LITTLETON

B4085

Start

SOUTH
LITTLETON

*Not to scale*

Follow the path out to the road in the housing estate and bear left. This is Middle Littleton. At the T-junction turn right and follow the road round the left-hand bend and at the next bend keep straight ahead. The huge tithe barn over to the right now belongs to the National Trust and can be visited. Built about 1300 and restored by the Trust in 1977 it has 11 bays, is partly aisled and the collar beams have short king posts. It is well worth a visit.

Continue the walk by going to a gate at the end of the track. From here bear right across the field to a stile in the right-hand hedge, 30 yards short of the far corner. In the next field turn left and follow the hedge on the left out to a lane. On the right is North Littleton. Bear left across the lane and go along the track opposite and continue for ½ mile, when the track turns left. Continue for ¼ mile to go over a footbridge and stile in the hedge in front. In the field turn right.

63

Now follow the hedge and later a fence on the right to join a track which will take you into Cleeve Prior.

At the main road turn left and walk through the village for ¼ mile. When the road starts to sweep round to the left turn right along Nightingale Lane and, in 200 yards, at the T-junction, turn right. At the end of the lane keep straight ahead through the field, next to the hedge on the left. Bear left across the metalled track and go down the path to a lane and turn left.

In a few yards bear right along the riverside path and, when the wood ends go through the fields, keeping near the river. In 1½ miles, keep to the left of a waterside cottage and continue past the weir. Walk on through the middle of a caravan site, down the service road and out to the B4510. Though not a busy road, cars tend to come hurtling down the hill from the left. Turn right and keep to the footpath. Just past the inn it is often possible to cross the river by the ford, although this is not a practice to be encouraged as a false step would mean being swept into deep water. It was a very important crossing until well into this century.

Continue along the road round the bend and in 100 yards turn left across the road, to walk along a stone track. At the top of the hill bear slightly right when the track forks and follow the hedge on the left for ½ mile to the church at South Littleton.

At the main road turn left and in 100 yards bear right to the start of the walk.

# KEMPSEY COMMON

## WALK 20

★

2½ miles (4 km)

OS Landranger 150, Pathfinder SO 84/94

This is an easy walk over the short turf of Kempsey Common and back through the old settlement of Stonehall.

Kempsey is on the A38(T), 3 miles south of Worcester. Its connections with river traffic have long since ceased and it has become a 'dormitory' for Worcester. It is now a large village and lacks the traditional village green. The parish is large and the common lies 2 miles south-east of the village. On a slight bend in the A38, ¾ mile south of the edge of the village, will be found signs indicating a lane to Napleton and Kempsey Common. In 1½ miles along this lane, just beyond the M5 Motorway, there is a large parking area in a corner of the common. This is where the walk starts. (GR: SO 866 483)

In the days—not so long ago—when each parish was responsible for its own poor, the parish boundary was most important and the 'beating of the bounds' was no insignificant tradition but was based on real economic necessity. Destitutes who could not be passed on to the next parish or sent back to the 'parish of birth' were likely to be a burden on the parish purse. This walk goes for some distance near the Kempsey boundary, a well-defined ditch across what was at one time grazing land for a number of parishes. In 1834 a stop was put to the granting of relief to able-bodied men (who had learnt to depend on it) and parishes were able to build workhouses and grant allotments. The Farmers Arms, on the right of the parking place, was once the Kempsey workhouse, and beyond it are the allotments, all taken out of common land.

Walk up the stone track away from the motorway. As you go up the hill the 20 acres hedged off from the common for allotments is on the right. Although now reduced in area it is still used by a few keen gardeners. Continue to the top of the first rise. If you turn round you see a good view of Worcester to the right and the Malverns to the left. As you go on up the common you gradually get closer to the parish boundary which is on your right: From the gate bear to the right of the track to cross the unfenced road and in a few yards turn left with the hedge on the right.

Walk on along the common to the right of the Fruiterers' Arms—

65

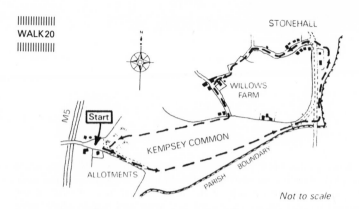

unless you wish to call there. In 200 yards bear left and continue along the road for 50 yards. Now turn left along a side road which is unfenced for the first 100 yards. This is the settlement of Stonehall, mentioned in 1275 as Stoneheath, so probably all this hill was once common grazing land. Walk on along the lane and beyond the last house go down a hedged track.

At the T-junction go to the left and in a few yards keep to the right-hand edge of the field. This is an old bridleway which was once a track. Since 1949, when a definitive map of rights of way was drawn up, each path in a parish has had a number. This is a bridleway, one degree higher than a footpath, and its number is 27. Some paths which go through a number of parishes keep changing their numbers as they cross the boundaries. Go through Willows Farm and at the lane, turn left and in 200 yards go through the gate on to the common again.

Turn right along the edge of the common and after passing the cottages, continue with the hedge on the right. When the hedge bears right keep straight ahead. Maintain this direction, going round the large patches of gorse from time to time, and you will soon come in sight of the beginning of the stone track where the walk started.

# POWICK

## WALK 21

★

3 miles (5 km)

OS Landranger 150, Pathfinder SO 85/95

Powick lies on the A449(T) road between Worcester and Malvern. Cars can be parked on the by-road near the old Powick bridge over the river Teme, on the Worcester side of the bridge. This loop of road is not signposted but can be seen from the new road and bridge which were built to relieve the old bridge of traffic. It was between here and ¼ mile downstream on the Worcester side of the Teme that the Battle of Worcester took place in 1651. (GR: SO 836 526)

Walk along the old road to the bridge. On the right is the building that was constructed at the turn of the century as the first hydro-electric power station in England, replacing a large flour mill. The electricity produced for Worcester and Malvern was DC and the riverside inn near the bridge in Worcester, called the Old Rectifying House, was where DC was converted to AC before distribution to the city.

Continue along the road for 200 yards to a gate on the right leading into Powick Ham. At the time of writing there is much talk of continuing the bypass from the island behind you across this meadow. Any new route will be well waymarked.

Cross this 'commonable land' by going just to the right of an electricity pylon and then to the left of an old loop of the river, now no more than a wide ditch. This is a fine example of an ox-bow or mortlake where a straighter channel has been cut, leaving the original channel to silt up. Bear right to a gate. From here the path goes across the meadow to the opposite hedge, 200 yards from the wood on the left and 100 yards to the right of a gate. Cross the stile and footbridge and walk down the middle of a very long meadow. At the far end there is a stile in the lower corner which leads into the bottom of a field. The right of way goes diagonally across to a pool, but local walkers usually tread a path round the edge—which is more interesting as it gives a close-up view of the river Teme. There used to be a number of houses dotted around here. You have passed the site of one in the long meadow but most were in the field behind the pool. The settlement was known as Piddlefields. The use of the archaic word piddle, which means 'small' or 'the lesser one', is

67

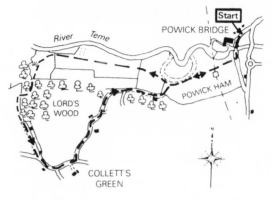

*Not to scale*

common in Worcestershire. There are a number of villages near Pershore with 'piddle' in their names.

Continue up to climb the stile into Lord's Wood and take the path ahead. Follow the old road down to Piddlefields on the right. In 100 yards turn right to a stile in the bottom corner of a field. Here turn left and go up, next to the wood, to a straight track. At the top of Lord's Wood there are a number of young elm trees. It is strange to remember that this rough-leaved tree used to be called the 'Worcestershire Weed' when every hedgerow had its row of suckers, each trying to become a 150 foot giant. In the eighteenth and nineteenth centuries, when the open fields were enclosed, landowners often insisted on elms being planted at intervals in the hawthorn hedges to provide timber and shelter.

Follow the track to a lane and bear left. In 200 yards turn left again along Kings End Road or Kings End Lane—both signs indicating the same way! Pass Collett's Green Farm, which has the appearance of a large timber-framed building that has been plastered over—a common practice since medieval times. In 100 yards turn left on to a track and, just past the last cottage on the left, keep to the track between hedges. Continue down the track to join another track at the bottom. Walk on along this track at the bottom of a wooded hillside, past a house and out into Powick Ham again. Bear left to join the route on which you came out and pass to the left of the pylon.

At the old road turn left back to the car.

# KNIGHTWICK

WALK 22

★

6 miles (9.5 km)

OS Landranger 150, Pathfinder SO 65/75

This walk provides magnificent views over the Severn valley to the east and the Herefordshire countryside into Wales to the west.

Knightwick is 7 miles west of Worcester and 16 miles from Leominster. The start of the walk is near Knightsford Bridge, on an old loop of the A44 road which went over a Teme bridge, now demolished and replaced by a footbridge. Cars can be parked on the southern section of the loop, which starts near the bus shelter on the A44, but not on the northern part near the foot of the hill by the Talbot Inn. (GR: SO 732 559)

From the bus shelter cross the main road to go along the side road. In 20 yards bear left towards Lulsley. After ¼ mile, when the lane starts to climb the hill, look for a gate into the last field on the left. Go through here and cross the field to the opposite corner, just below the wood. Bear right between the river and the wood and you come eventually into the end of a long meadow. Follow the hedge on the right for nearly ½ mile, to a gate in the corner.

Bear right in the field beyond for 100 yards, passing the end of the barns, and then go left to a track in front of the buildings. This is the start of the lane past Lulsley Court, a magnificent timber-framed building on the left at the far end of the outbuildings. Lull was an Old English personal name but it lost an 'l' in the eighteenth century. Walk on along the lane past the farm on the right called Cold Place: Cold is usually a distortion of Colles, a family name. Continue along the lane for ½ mile, passing the inhabited church and at the road junction bear right. The house that you now see on the right used to be Knightwick railway station.

Just over the brow of the hill turn left up a sunken track. In 200 yards keep straight ahead, passing to the right of a cottage. Keep near the hedge in the field at the end of the track. In the corner go through a gate on to the track again as it goes through the edge of a wood. All the way along the top of this ridgeway you are following an ancient trackway, which can only be recognised from time to time.

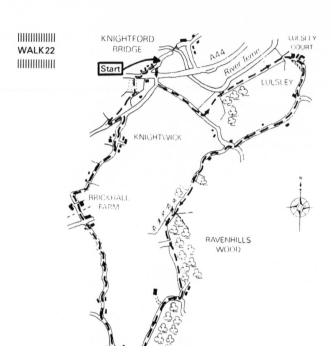

||||||||||||||||
**WALK 22**
||||||||||||||||

KNIGHTFORD
BRIDGE

Start

A44

River Teme

LULSLEY
COURT

LULSLEY

KNIGHTWICK

BRICKHALL
FARM

RAVENHILLS
WOOD

N

*Not to scale*

In the next field follow the hedge again and at the far end go through the right-hand gate into another short length of woodland. When going through the next field keep near the wood on the left and then go through two gates in quick succession: you are now in the wood. To the left is the Ravenshill Nature Reserve, the entrance to which is on the other side of the wood.

Follow the path until it comes out on to a track. Walk down the track to the lane and turn right over the hill.

Continue along the lane down the hill. At the bottom of the hill pass a turning to the left to Longley Green and in a further ¼ mile turn right up a track and, in a few yards, pass a black and white house on the right. Keep to this track, which is an unmaintained council road, as it winds between hedges for ¾ mile. Pass Highfields Farm on the right and cross the lane. A short way past the bridge over the old railway cutting, keep to the left of Brickhall Farm with its new buildings on the left and go down to a gate. Here the track goes down the side of a field to sweep round and continue into Knightwick. It is a settlement with a long history for it is first mentioned in a Saxon charter where the name 'cnihts-wic' implies that it was a dairy farm run by a group of men, possibly war veterans who had been rewarded with an enterprise to be run in common.

Keep to the lane past the church and go down to the road. Here turn left for 100 yards and then double back through a gate on the right to enter a field. Walk down the centre of the field to pass to the left of some bushes. A grass track can be seen on the hillside in front. Follow this round to an orchard and from here go between the trees to a stile in the road fence. The bus shelter can be seen down the A44 to the right. Walk down the road verge until the footway starts on the opposite side and then cross with care.

# ABBOTS MORTON

## WALK 23

★

6½ or 8½ miles (10.5 or 13.5 km)

OS Landranger 150, Pathfinder SP 05/15

This walk is from the Ridgeway down into the valley of the river Arrow. Should you wish to continue into Alcester, a route has been described to this interesting town which, because it lies just off the main road, is little affected by modern traffic.

Cars can be parked on a gravel lay-by at the side of a minor road which goes through Weethley Wood at a point called Morton Spirt. It can best be reached from near the southern end of the A441, ¾ mile from its junction with the A435, which is just south of Ragley Hall. Take the road to Worcester at the sharp bend with the old toll house and follow this minor road for ¾ mile. (GR: SP 046 545)

Walk on along the road towards Worcester, over the brow of the hill and down past the black and white cottages. Turn right into the first big field on the right. Walk along next to the hedge on the right for ½ mile, going through three fields. In a corner, where the wood widens out a few yards, you will see an old hunting gateway on the right leading into the wood. Go through this and follow the path up through the wood, across a muddy ride at the top and out at the far side on the edge of a large field. Continue ahead across the field, crossing the ditch by an overgrown stone bridge, and making for a solitary tree in the middle of the field. From here the stile lies straight ahead.

Climb the stile and make for the two gates on the far side of the field, turning left here to follow the fenced ditch on the right until you reach a farm gate. In the absence of a stile you may need to climb the gate. Keep to the right of the field by the hedge until you reach a stile and stone track. Turn left and in 100 yards turn right over a stile in the hedge and follow the path up into a field. Go on up to the lane at Weethley.

As you come across the valley you will have noticed a little church on the hill with five neighbouring dwellings. These former farm buildings, which once seemed destined for use as hard-core, have been superbly renovated and now make up Weethley hamlet.

Turn left along the lane to the main road which follows the line of an

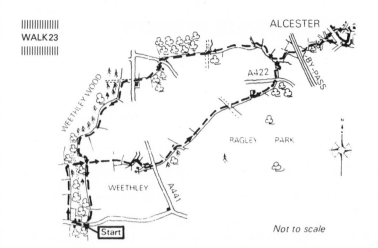

ancient trackway running along the Ridgeway. Once used by pack-horses and travellers on foot it is now used by travellers going thirty times faster encased in 20 cwt containers! So cross with care to the stile next to the gate. Pass into the field and follow the boundary of Ragley Park, on the right, down through two fields. Ragley Hall can be seen only when there are no leaves on the trees. Just past an old barn bear right to a stile and continue to follow the park boundary for 1 mile.

When you come to a derelict farm, turn right and pass the old buildings on your left. Keep straight ahead, next to the fence on the right, as far as the main road. Because of the bend to your right, it is best to cross here and walk along the verge to the right for 50 yards, as far as the first gateway. Go in here and follow the hedge with its hidden ditch to a stile in the corner. In the field beyond turn left and make your way to a gate. Take care when using this gate as it swings out over the edge of the farm bridge.

If you wish to return to the car from this point turn left and miss out the next 2 paragraphs. Should you wish to go on the longer walk, into Alcester, turn right.

Follow the ditch on the right for 100 yards and where the ditch bends to the right turn left along the edge of the field, having the hedge on the right. At the corner turn right into a large field, which is divided by the Alcester bypass. Make your way diagonally across the field along the well-trodden footpath, crossing the dual carriageway with care. Continue in the same direction to a wooden footbridge over Spittle Brook. Keep straight ahead to a stile and a rectangular field. Cross to the opposite corner, follow the path out to the road and turn left.

73

At the crossroads go straight over and bear right to a path between gardens (No Cycling). Bear left across the main road to go down a path at the side of the inn opposite. Follow this path through the park and on the road beyond turn left for 10 yards and then right. This will bring you into the centre of Alcester. To return, go to the large traffic island where the Evesham road meets the Redditch–Stratford road. Go along Seggs Lane, which is just to the right of the Evesham Road and in 300 yards, at the crossroads, turn left along Roman Way. Now retrace your steps until you are walking by the side of the ditch.

Follow the ditch on your left and in the field beyond the second hedge go round the field to a stile, just past the first corner. Cross the narrow brick bridge and keep ahead next to the hedge on the left for ½ mile. In the far corner cross the ditch to a stone track, on which turn left and in a few paces turn right so as to walk with the hedge on the right. This will bring you to a length of main road which remained when straightening took place. Go on to the present road and cross to go up the drive towards Thornhill House. Keep straight ahead and pass the barn to go round to the right just beyond a wooden shed. From the field gate bear left up the hill, next to the wood. Pass through another field gate on the left and, keeping the hedge on the right, go to a small gate in the top right-hand corner of the field. This leads to the main Ridgeway road. Cross to the gate opposite and follow the track towards the wood but just before reaching it turn left along the edge of the field.

The footpath now follows the edge of the wood for 1¾ miles to the lane, a few yards from the car. At the bottom of the third field cross the ditch and continue by the side of the wood. In a further ½ mile you will pass the place where you came out of the wood on your way to Weethley.

On reaching the lane turn right, back to the car.

# THORNBURY

WALK 24

★

4 miles (6.5 km)

OS Landranger 149, Pathfinder SO 65/75

Climbing easily to the top of a ridge dominated by a large prehistoric settlement, this walk has many fine views across the surrounding countryside.

Thornbury is little more than a handful of houses, 4 miles north-west of Bromyard. It is reached by turning off the B4214 Bromyard–Tenbury Wells road 3 miles north of Bromyard. Cars can be parked 1½ miles along this side road on the grass verge, ¼ mile south of the church, where the bank on the inside of a large bend has been removed. (GR: SO 623 593)

Walk on along the road past the lane to the church. In a further 200 yards go down to turn right along a 'No Through Road' to Pool House. After ¼ mile pass the farm with its pool on the left and keep ahead, going to the left of the garden hedge belonging to a bungalow.

Go through a gate in front and walk with the field hedge on the left. At the next corner pass through the left of two gates and now walk with a hedge on the right. From the next gate continue, with first a fence and then a hedge on the left, to the corner where there is a gate on the left. In the next field go forward for 100 yards to the corner and then turn right and follow the hedge on the left round two full sides of the field to a gate in the corner. Beyond here a track to the left starts, which crosses the brook and then goes up to cross a field. Follow this track but in the field go straight ahead to pass to the right of an old farm called Kyrebatch.

The bridlepath you are following goes to the field gate ahead. At the time of writing the outbuildings of the farmhouse are being turned into modern houses and it may be necessary to continue up the track to a gate in the new fence and turn right round the buildings to the field gate.

How sad it is to see an old timber-framed house such as this fall into disrepair. One can imagine how it must have looked 100 years ago when it was the centre of much human and animal activity. It is perhaps fortunate that they can be preserved in a different form rather than disappearing completely. Beyond the field gate there used to be a

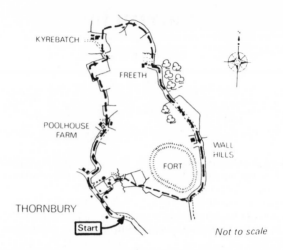

KYREBATCH

FREETH

POOLHOUSE
FARM

WALL
HILLS

FORT

THORNBURY

Start

*Not to scale*

number of smaller fields so that is why the bridleway goes ahead for 50 yards before turning right to pass behind a large oak tree. If you look carefully you can still see the course of the old track going just to the left of the corner. On nearing the corner, bear right to a gate and then follow the faint track up the hill to a second gate. Now follow the hedge on the left to a stone track near a small farm with the name of Freeth, turn left and follow the track—which gradually improves.

When you reach the top of the hill there are fine views to Great Witley and the Ankerdine Hills. Rain falling on the left of the lane drains north-west to Tenbury Wells and, *via* the river Teme, reaches the Severn at Worcester; whilst rain falling to the right gets eventually to the Severn at Chepstow, having gone *via* the Frome and Wye.

Continue along the lane past the high ramparts of Wall Hills, a pre-Roman camp extending to over 15 acres. The lane continues round the southern end of the hill fort and then turns left. In 100 yards there is a gate into the field on the right. Go through this and follow the edge of the field round to a stile on the right 100 yards along the second boundary. This takes you up into a long field below the impressive fortifications of the fort. Turn left and follow the fence on the left. When the fence turns left keep straight ahead rising slightly to eventually go down to a stile. This takes you into the corner of a field. Keeping near the left-hand boundary go down to another stile. The footpath now goes diagonally down the field to a track and bridge over a stream—the little river Frome. From here straight ahead up to a gate into the churchyard. The nave is Norman, the tower thirteenth century, but the chancel 1865.

Walk down the lane from the church and turn left back to the car.

# GRIMLEY

## WALK 25

★

3½ miles (5.5 km)

OS Landranger 150, Pathfinder SO 85/95, 86/96

Grimley village is situated ½ mile from the A443 Worcester–Tenbury road, 4 miles north of Worcester. Make for the northern end of an elbow-shaped loop of the A443, which was left when a ¼ mile straight length of road was made to bypass it. Near a small red post box there is a very wide grass verge which is suitable for parking the car. The walk starts by going through a small kissing gate next to the post box. (GR: SO 829 605)

The ridge from which the walk starts has extensive gravel beds, laid down when northern England was covered with ice as far south as Wolverhampton. This walk is in an area which was favoured by early settlers, but because gravel is in demand today for building and road works it is being quarried, so destroying—for ever—the faint traces left by our predecessors. The sketch map on page 00 has been extended to show some of these traces which could only be seen on aerial photographs. Photographs taken in 1960 and 1968 reveal the corner of a Roman fort in the field to the north of the church but nothing else has been seen in the adjoining field as it is permanently under grass and the church and houses cover the remainder so the size of the fort is unknown. Two straight roads can just be detected leading to it, however, and various enclosures and boundary ditches can be seen on some photographs (of which more than 50 were taken between 1956 and 1971) and much of the higher land has ridge and furrow marks. The circles are barrows which have been flattened and ploughed over.

After going through the kissing gate next to the post box aim across the field just to the left of Grimley Church tower. Cross the low ground from which the gravel has been extracted and go up into the corner of a field, then follow the fence on the left into the field next to the churchyard. This is the area of the Roman fort and the only known corner is in the field to the left of the houses. Bear right to enter the churchyard by a kissing gate and follow the path past the church to the road. Here turn left, past the Waggon Wheels inn and follow the lane down to the right until you reach the river. A few yards from the river turn right over a footbridge and stile to walk along the river bank.

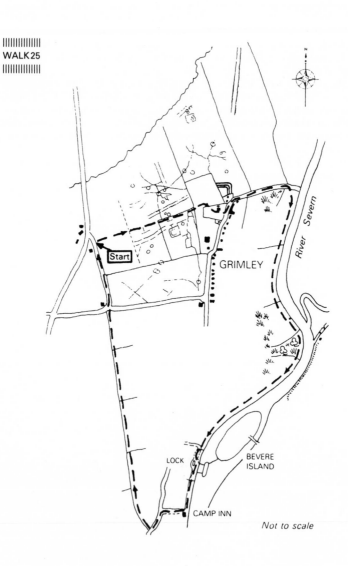

WALK 25

Start

GRIMLEY

River Severn

LOCK

BEVERE
ISLAND

CAMP INN

Not to scale

In ½ mile, about 100 yards before reaching a wood, look for a round metal mile-post reading 'to Stourport 8½ miles' and standing 1 foot high in the grass a few yards from the river bank. Pass through the small wood to arrive at Bevere Lock. From Bevere Island have come Celtic and Roman relics and it is to this spot that the citizens of Worcester have flocked on many occasions—to avoid the vengeance of Hardicanute for not paying Danegeld, for instance, or to escape the dreaded plague of 1637.

Walk on past the lock to the attractive Camp Inn, an eighteenth century service station when the river was busy with traffic. Turn right by the side of the building and continue up the drive to the sharp right-hand bend. Here turn left along a hedged track. In 100 yards, when the track bears left, turn right into the corner of the field which has been on your right.

Follow the hedge on the left for ¾ mile to the elbow of old road in which the walk started, 300 yards ahead.

# SHELSLEY BEAUCHAMP

WALK 26

★

5½ miles (9 km)

OS Landranger 149, 150, Pathfinder SO 66, 76

Shelsley Beauchamp lies 7 miles north-west of Worcester on the banks of the river Teme. From the A443 at Great Witley, go south on the B4197 towards Martley and take the second turn on the right. From Martley take the B4204 road towards Tenbury Wells and in 1½ miles turn right. In 1 mile turn right again. Cars can be parked on the grass verge 100 yards towards Shelsley Beauchamp from Newmill Bridge over the river Teme. (GR: SO 730 625)

Walk down the road and cross Newmill Bridge. The two cottages on the left have lost their thatch but the tiling is very well done. What fun they must have had with the eyebrows!

Turn right at the junction and continue along the lane to the village of Shelsley Walsh. Turn left up to the church. The church of St Andrew has a Norman nave and a thirteenth century chancel. It is built of tufa. Along this hillside there are many streams issuing from the limestone. They have the property of forming tufa, a deposit produced from a solution of calcium bicarbonate. Under a change of temperature and pressure, calcium carbonate is deposited on twigs and stones over which the water flows. Large deposits were once formed, enough to quarry and build the church. It is popular with builders who can cut it very easily when freshly mined.

Walk along the lane opposite the church and turn left up the hill. There is a footpath along the road up the hill but it may be closed on one Sunday in the year because this is where they hold a hill-climb for cars. As you go up you will see the places in the bank for the timing devices, the seats in the 'grandstand' and the television tower on the inside of the bend.

On reaching the barns at the top continue ahead to join a stone track which turns right. Pass to the right side of a cottage to follow a sunken track to a gate in the top corner of the field. Walk on for 100 yards and at the T-junction of tracks turn left. As you go through the kissing gate by the side of the farm gate at the end of the field notice the roots curiously convoluted in the bank at the side of the gate.

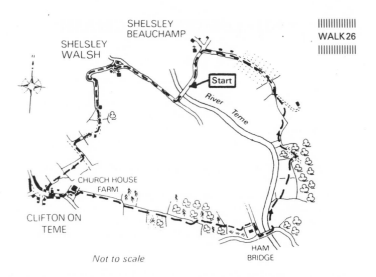

Start

River Teme

CHURCH HOUSE
FARM

CLIFTON ON
TEME

HAM
BRIDGE

*Not to scale*

Turn right, leaving the track to go straight ahead and cross in front of an old sports pavilion. Walk to the right-hand gate in front. In the next field go straight ahead to the opposite hedge, a few yards from the corner, where there is a stile. Now follow the hedge on the left as it curves round to the left, to walk through a garden, past a new house and down the drive to the road at Clifton on Teme, a medieval 'New Town' which failed!

On the opposite side of the road to the church is the old smithy. Repairs to coaches and waggons were carried out in the left half, the part with the horseshoe over the arch, while the shoeing was done behind the stable door to the right. As you will see, there are many black and white houses around the attractive village green, along to the right. It should be noted that although you have now climbed 500 feet from the river Teme this place is called Clifton *on* Teme!

Walk along the road, with the church on your left, for 200 yards and turn left at the entrance to Church Farm. A few yards up the drive turn right and join a bridleway, a track round a pond and along the side of a field, next to the hedge on the left. This bridleway will go downhill for over a mile until it reaches the road near the river. In ¼ mile, as you pass to the right of a wood, look at the view. The hills over to the right are the Malverns, seen end on; the near ridge just across the Teme valley is Ankerdine Hill; and just to its left is dome-shaped Bredon, standing out in the Vale of Evesham.

In a further ½ mile follow the path through the wood to the left and

81

then go round the field to the right to a gate on to the road where you turn right. At a T-junction turn left and cross Ham Bridge. On the far side you will see a footpath sign to the left. Follow this path through two fields into a water meadow at the far end of which follow the track up into the wood and, at the sharp right-hand bend, turn left. At the end of the wood go through the gate in front and cross the narrow end of a meadow. Continue up the hill keeping beside the hedge on the right. Go through the first gate and turn left, still following the hedge, to a track down from the now empty Lower House Farm and keep to this track till you reach the church at Shelsley Beauchamp.

Turn left down the road back to the car.

# SHRAWLEY

## WALK 27

★

7 miles (11 km)

OS Landranger 150, Pathfinder SO 86/96

The walk starts from an old loop of road outside the Lenchford Inn on the B4196 Worcester–Stourport road. The Lenchford is ¾ mile north of Holt Heath, a scattered village where the A4133 crosses the B4196. Cars can be parked anywhere along this length of road. (GR: SO 813 643)

Walk up the hill along the road towards Shrawley. In ¼ mile turn right through a gate next to a footpath sign and follow the track just below the wood. At the end of the wood bear left to a stile at the side of a gate and in the next field turn right by the hedge. In the corner of the field go through a gate and in the field beyond keep the same direction to a stile and footbridge in the opposite hedge. In 200 yards bear right over a marshy patch to continue with the wood on the left and a lagoon on the right. Ten yards past the next stile turn left on to a narrow path into the wood. Just inside the wood turn right. Follow this path up into Shrawley Wood.

At the top of the rise walk ahead, along a grassed forest road, for ¼ mile. The large trees you pass on the left are Wellingtonias, interesting trees first imported from California in 1853. They make extremely rapid and continuous growth and in the Sierra Nevada specimens have been found over 328 feet high and 88 feet round. Wellingtonias are said to live for more than 3,000 years, so these near Shrawley are mere saplings. They never seem to blow down but, as you may guess, their greatest enemy is lightning. The bark is so thick and soft that you can punch it without damaging yourself.

At the second small dip in the path there is a cross-track, turn right and go downhill on a forest road to a footbridge over Dick Brook. Stay here for a while and look round at the peaceful countryside. The woods and pastures show little sign of anything but the seasonal activities of the farming community. It was not so 300 years ago. At the time when the Civil War was engaging the energies of the extremists and when London was being rebuilt after the Great Fire, this quiet backwater saw one of the bursts of experimentation which led to the industrial revolution. Andrew Yarrangton, who was born 1½ miles upstream from this

GLASSHAMPTON MONASTERY

DICK FORGE THE

BROOK

YARRANGTON'S FURNACE

B4196

River

CLACK'S FARM

SHRAWLEY

Severn

Start

THE LENCHFORD

*Not to scale*

spot, was foremost in the development of iron working and tin plating. He travelled extensively and wrote books with grand titles such as *The Improvement of England by Sea and Land*. A mile away, up Dick Brook, he set up a furnace and used the brook to transport thousands of tons of cinders which were rich in iron and which had been discarded by the Romans on the bank of the Severn at Worcester. The cinders were brought from there, up river to the wharf at the mouth of the brook, across the field to the right, where they were transhipped into small barges or tub-boats and, with the aid of two locks, taken upstream.

Continue the walk by crossing the narrow field and turning left along a cart-track up the valley, having a wooded ridge on the right. At the end of the field there are the remains of a cottage on the right. Just beyond on the left is an overgrown hollow, this is the site of the forge, a profitable concern, and also thought to be the site of Yarrangton's successful experiments in tin plating. In later years the forge ground flint for the Worcester porcelain industry. The water for the overshot wheel which drove the bellows came down a leat in the valley on the right and then passed under the track on which you are standing.

Follow the track up the valley as far as the road and then turn left. Cross the bridge and turn right along a private road to Glasshampton Monastery. Past the lodge, away to the left across the field in the wood, is the site of Yarrangton's furnace. It was exposed when a dam burst some years ago but has since become completely overgrown. Follow the stone track for ½ mile. Ahead will be seen a handsome brick building and this is Glasshampton Monastery, the first Anglican Cistercian house. The block was built in the early nineteenth century as the stables for Glasshampton House which stood at the top of the field in front, to the left of the stables, but was destroyed by fire soon after it was built. The site of the mansion can just be seen as a flat area in the middle of the field. Glasshampton gets its name from a stream, Glasa—the Anglo-Saxon for bright or clear—and is mentioned in the Domesday Book.

At the foot of the hill which goes up to the monastery the main track turns left towards Woolstans Farm. Follow this track to the left and in 300 yards, when the track turns sharp right, go straight ahead through a gate. In the field maintain the same direction down to a stile which takes you over the dam of Upper Nutnell Pool. This is the same sort of dam which covered Yarrangton's furnace at the far end of Lower Nutnell Pool. In the field beyond, the bridle path you have been following goes straight across to the right-hand corner and then on for 1½ miles to Little Witley. From the far corner of the field a footpath crosses over to the left. A number of hedges have been removed here and the fields have changed from grass to arable so, in the interests of the farmer, go round the left-hand edge of the field to the end of the wood and then turn left. Keep ahead along an old fence and climb up past the end of a wood on the right.

Follow the hedge on the right to the top of the second field, where there is a gate. In the next field go to the left round the edge for about 200 yards to a gate in the corner from which you can see Bonefield's Farm up to the left. The footpath goes straight across the field to cross one coming down from the farm. Go to this and turn right, with your back to the farm. Climb a fence and go up the field with the hedge on the right.

Beyond the next field gate turn right to a stile in a fence and then left up to the right of a barn. Cross the stile in front into a field, turn left next to the hedge and just past the garden of the cottage turn left over a stile to a drive and turn right. Continue along a lane to a T-junction.

Turn right and follow this quiet lane for ½ mile and, 10 yards before it joins the main road at a sharp bend, turn right into the bottom of a field. Now follow the fence on the left up to a gate, about half way up the hill, then turn left and go towards the far right-hand corner in front of the church. Turn right through a small gate in the corner and follow the path into the churchyard. At the church turn right out to the road.

Turn left along the road past the old well-head, still with its winding gear, set back in the churchyard wall. At the bend turn right through the first gate and follow the hedge on the left. In the next field look down the field to the bottom hedge for a tall oak tree, 200 yards from the left-hand corner. Go down the slope at the back of the tree, across the stream and out into the field beyond. Climb up the field to follow the hedge on the left to the third gate. Go through and bear right across the corner of the field to a stile 50 yards from the corner of a garden wall. This stile will take you into the small parkland of Severnbank House, in which go forward down to the cattle-grid and so out to the B4196.

Cross the road and turn left along the grass verge, back to the car.

# HANBURY

## WALK 28

★

4 miles (6.5 km)

OS Landranger 150, Pathfinder SO 96

The walk starts from the northern end of a wood called Dodderhill Common which stands on Piper's Hill, ½ mile north of the village of Hanbury. From Bromsgrove go south on the A38 and then the B4091 for 4 miles. From Droitwich go east along the B4090 (The Salt Way) for 4 miles and turn left through Hanbury for 1½ miles. From Alcester take the B4090 westwards for 8½ miles and turn right through the village of Hanbury. Cars may be parked under the trees, just inside the wood. (GR: SO 958 651)

Walk on down the track through the parking area, round the lake and past Knotts Farm. In a further 200 yards there is a narrow path down through the bushes on the right which goes to a section of metal fence acting as a stile in the hedge at the edge of the wood and leads into the corner of a field. Go down the field, with the hedge on the left, to a stile, 20 yards from the bottom corner. From here walk on, still with a hedge on the left. In the corner of the next field there is a stile in the hedge on the left and, on the other side of it, an overgrown track and another hedge. Bear right to a second stile.

These double hedges were very common in districts where stock was raised, as it enabled the farmer to drive animals from a distant field to the farm without going through the intermediate fields, an important point if these fields had stock in them or were 'up' for hay. Today a temporary electric fence can be erected in a few minutes, so the old hedged tracks have become overgrown.

Continue along the edge of the field to the corner where there is a stile and a meeting of tracks. Cross straight over to another stile and walk with the hedge on the right for ½ mile to a lane. Bear right across this lane to a gate and from here go straight ahead to another gate on the other side of the field. There used to be a hedge for you to follow but this has gone the way of so many hedges. In the next field keep near the hedge on the left through two fields and then a stile will lead you up a short bank on to the towing path of the Worcester and Birmingham Canal.

87

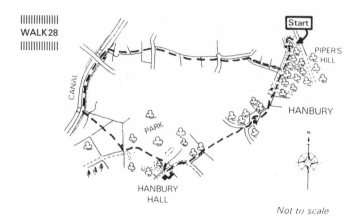

PIPER'S HILL

HANBURY

CANAL

PARK

HANBURY HALL

N

*Not to scale*

At its northern end the canal goes into the very heart of Birmingham but to reach there from Worcester involves climbing 400 feet through 58 locks. The canal was completed in 1815 but within 30 years a railway from Birmingham to Gloucester had taken most of its traffic. The last load of coal from Cannock to Worcester passed in 1960, the last load of chocolate crumb to Cadburys at Bournville in 1961. Today the waterway is busy again with pleasure cruisers.

Turn left along the canal and pass the keeper's cottage at the first lock. At the second lock, in ¼ mile, turn left and go over a stile in the hedge and cross straight over the narrow field to a new metal footbridge. From here the right of way goes along the hedge on the left for 100 yards and then bears slightly right, crossing a fence 100 yards from the hedge and going on to the far corner of the field. If this field is under mowing grass people usually tread a path slightly to the right, to a gate and then along a fence to a track and turn left on another footpath; both routes arrive at the same place, which is near a small shed.

Go into Hanbury Park and straight ahead from the gate for 100 yards. Now look over to the right for a small round clump of trees at the foot of a bank and cross the park to go just to the left of these trees. From the high fence in front, the footpath goes up to a drive through what is now an arable field but was once parkland. At the time of writing this is impassable, so go a few yards to the right, up the bank to a gate and turn left along the drive for 100 yards to join the correct line of the footpath.

Hanbury Hall was built about 1700, possibly by Talman, the architect responsible also for Chatsworth. The Hall, a very fine example of the country house of that period, is now owned by the National Trust.

88

Walk along the drive and at the sharp right-hand bend keep straight ahead, through what used to be an avenue of oak trees. From the stile into the next field keep the same direction up to a stile and on to a lane. On the left you will see the ruins of a coach house. When the family from the great house came to church the coach and horses were stabled here during the somewhat lengthy service.

This is 'Archers' country. Some of the episodes for this daily radio programme have been recorded in Hanbury Church. The inn at Inkberrow, 5 miles south-east of here, added a name to the series and has its uses when the cast is out on location. Godfrey Baseley, who helped to create the Archers, and many of the original cast came from this area.

Pass to the left of the church and bear left to a small gate. Continue along the path down the side of the hill and go through a gate, to walk along beside the hedge on the right. Enter the wood and pass a massive oak tree, then bear left to a narrow but well-used path which will take you back to Knotts Farm.

Continue past the lake and up the hill to the parking place.

# WYRE FOREST

## WALK 29

★

5 miles (8 km)

OS Landranger 138, Pathfinder SO 67/77

The Wyre Forest has long been a mecca for Midlanders seeking a quiet walk. The route here described explores some of the less frequented parts. It has somewhat miraculously managed to preserve its rural character despite the fact that it contains workable seams of coal. In the early days of the Industrial Revolution in the eighteenth century the river Severn although acting as a means of communication also acted as a barrier. In contrast to Ironbridge, Wyre lacked the initiative and foresight of an Abraham Darby, even though it was equally well endowed with coal and iron.

The walk starts from the Forestry Commission's Wyre Forest Visitors Centre which is off the A456 road, 2 miles west of Bewdley. It is well signposted. (GR: SO 750 739)

Leave the parking area and go down the wide forest road. These modern forest roads have many benefits, such as the creation of open spaces for butterflies, allowing the movement of wildlife along their verges and the provision of corridors linking key sites. In ¼ mile, when the forest road can be seen to go up ahead and there is a narrow track going off to the right, turn left up a path which rises steeply. In nearly ¼ mile there is a meeting of tracks on the edge of a wide forest road. A forest path comes in from the right, it is along here that you will come on the way back. Ahead, at the T-junction with a wide forest road, turn right.

Continue along the forest road gradually losing height and in a little over 1 mile there is a driveway on the left leading to a cottage with the warning 'Beware Guard Dogs'. Here the track turns sharp right. Just before the bend you passed a cross-track which was the line of the old railway which ran between Tenbury Wells and Kidderminster. In its later days it had railcoaches and when they reached this point the driver switched off the engine and the coach glided quietly—sometimes in a valley, sometimes above the trees—down into Kidderminster.

Walk on down the forest road, across the footbridge and turn right to continue along the valley of the Dowles Brook. This quiet wooded place

*Not to scale*

was once the scene of great industrial activity. Until the seventeenth century the only way to work iron was to heat it in a charcoal fire, so furnaces and forges were sited near forests where charcoal could be made. A good stream was also necessary to drive the hammers and bellows and float the pigs up from, and the finished products down to, a riverside wharf. This was an ideal place and 300 years ago the scene was very different but unlike the Forest of Dean it failed to change with the times.

In ¼ mile, on reaching the wide junction of tracks, cross the small stream and turn right following the waymarked bridleway. Continue with this path, on first one side and then the other of the brook. As you go through the forest you may notice piles of very small twigs; these are the nests of wood ants. It is not unusual to find an ant, ¼ inch long, carrying a twig 20 times its own length and sometimes, if you bend down to look at one closely, it will stop what it was doing and rear up ready to fight you—I think I should be reluctant to take on a giant twice as high as the tallest tree!

When you see that the path ahead goes down steeply, turn right to go up a horse track—denoted by a horseshoe burnt into the top of a post. This leads out to a wide track where you turn right. This is the disused railway again. After ¼ mile it is crossed by an old horse track, one of the old forest roads. Horses were able to work in much rougher conditions than the modern tractor, which needs a more solid and fairly smooth surface if it is not to sink into the ground. A team of four horses with their 16 hooves pressing down had much better traction than a tractor with two spinning wheels. Consequently, many of the old forest roads have been either abandoned or widened and re-surfaced beyond all recognition.

Turn left onto the old track and go up into the wood. Crossing a modern forest road continue in the same general direction for nearly 1 mile. There are a number of cross-tracks and branches off which should be ignored, always pressing onwards and upwards.

Soon after crossing a marshy stream bed the path comes out on to a wide forest road. Cross straight over and follow a narrower and older forest track. In 200 yards there are seats in a small glade. In the middle is the 'Sorb Tree'. This is the Whitty pear—it has pear-like flowers and fruit but an ash-like leaf. It is a native of Southern Europe and North Africa so why is it here? We do not know, but its parent was recorded in 1678, and it was an old tree then. This tree, planted in 1913, is a direct descendant of the original Whitty pear of Wyre.

Continue along the well trodden path which eventually comes out at the T-junction you were at on the way out. Here turn left and retrace the route back to the wide forest road where a right turn will soon bring the car park into view.

# TRIMPLEY

## WALK 30

★

3 miles (5 km)

OS Landranger 138, Pathfinder SO 67/77

This walk starts high above the river Severn and goes down through woods and fields to Upper Arley where it is possible to cross the river and visit the railway station, which has been restored to its previous glory. A trip on a steam train can be taken from here to Bridgnorth or Bewdley and then the walk resumed through woods.

The Severn Valley Railway runs the 16 miles between Kidderminster and Bridgnorth. It is a steam operated, standard gauge railway, run by very competent volunteers. There are six stations and tickets (first or third class) can be obtained for a round tour. The main engine sheds are at Bridgnorth, which is an interesting and unique town—or rather two towns, one set high on a sandstone ridge, the other nestling at its foot—and well worth a visit. Trains run between March and October but the timetable varies; they run only at weekends at the beginning and end of the season, but from mid-May to the end of September there is a frequent daily service. Full information which includes a timetable for the year can be obtained from Severn Valley Railway, The Railway Station, Bewdley, Worcestershire DY12 1BG, telephone 0299 403816. (There is also a 'talking timetable' on 0299 401001.)

Trimpley is a small village 2 miles north-west of Kidderminster. It is best reached from the A456 road on the edge of Bewdley by turning on to the B4190 road, ¼ mile east of Wribbenhall Church. About ¼ mile along the B4190 turn left along Trimpley Lane and follow the signs to Trimpley. The road becomes steep and narrow, so drive with care. In ¼ mile beyond a minor crossroads at the top of the hill turn left at the sign for Trimpley Church and Elmore Wood. Continue along this road for 1 mile until the public road ends at a set of gates, beyond which the road is private.

There is a car park on the left just above the footpath sign you will come back to at the end of the walk. Should the area be already full of cars (for this is a popular place) there is plenty of space in the two large lengths of old road, a little way back up the hill. (GR: SO 775 792)

Start the walk by turning right at the end of the public road, along a

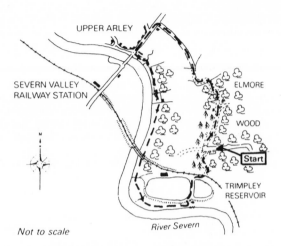

UPPER ARLEY

SEVERN VALLEY
RAILWAY STATION

ELMORE

WOOD

Start

TRIMPLEY
RESERVOIR

*Not to scale*

*River Severn*

track signposted 'Bridleway, Arley 1'. Follow this good track and in 200 yards go straight over the cross-tracks. Continue through the wood and when you come to the foresters' sheds on the left keep straight ahead, leaving the main track to go up to the right. After crossing over a wooden bridge and passing through a gate, the track is between fences over the open hill. On the way down there is an old hedge on the right. At the road, cross with care and turn left. (As this is a rather narrow lane remember to walk facing the oncoming traffic.) Go down into Upper Arley where there used to be an important ford and, until recently, a ferry. The new footbridge enables pedestrians to cross the river in much greater comfort than in earlier years. Those who wish to visit the railway station should cross the river and go up the lane past the Harbour Inn. Return and cross the bridge.

From the end of the footbridge the path goes along the riverside just below the houses. It is well used by fishermen, who find this reach of the river very productive. Follow the track for ½ mile and go under a railway bridge and continue to a stile leading out of the wood. In the field beyond go forward for 50 yards and then bear left to cross a farm bridge and so come back to the bank of the river again. On nearing a small railed-off part of the river bank with a modern building up to the left, turn left up a flight of wooden steps. This brings you to Trimpley Reservoir. If you are lucky you will find the water covered with dozens of small sailing craft belonging to a local sailing club. The public right of way actually went a little further down stream and round the smaller lake but you will see a notice at the top of the bank which says, 'The footpath on this embankment is for your enjoyment . . .' However, as most people walk the short distance from the road through the wood on the opposite side down to this pleasant spot, all the notices face away from you.

Continue round to the right and then go down between the reservoir and the smaller lake—the 'sludge lagoon'. Halfway round the second side of the lagoon turn left through a gate to the railway. Remember your highway code; stop, look and listen. If you hear or see no steam trains, cross the lines and enter the wood. In a few yards you will see you are on an old track, parts of which still show clearly that the stone surface was carefully laid by hand. In 100 yards bear left and follow the track, with the oak wood on the right.

You soon come out on to the end of the public road where the walk started.